ANDREW FROST

Andrew Frost is a writer and broadcaster. His articles have been published in a variety of Australian and international contemporary art and film publications and he is a regular contributor to the *Sydney Morning Herald*. In 2007 he wrote and presented *The Art Life*, a series on Australian contemporary art, and its sequel *The Art Life 2* (2009), and TV specials including *The Venice Biennale* (2007) and *In Conversation: Brian Eno* (2009). His fiction has been published in a number of journals and magazines including *I'm Worse at What I Do Best*, *Runway*, *Iceberg Journal* and *Global Short Stories*. He lives on the Central Coast of NSW.

For Lily

AUSTRALIAN SCREEN CLASSICS

the boys

ANDREW FROST

CURRENCY PRESS,
SYDNEY

First published by Currency Press Pty Ltd and the Australian Film Commission in 2010.

Currency Press Pty Ltd
PO Box 2287, Strawberry Hills
NSW 2012 Australia
enquiries@currency.com.au
www.currency.com.au

National Film and Sound Archive
A division of the Australian Film Commission
GPO Box 2002, Canberra
ACT 2601 Australia
www.nfsa.afc.gov.au

Australian Screen Classics series: ISSN 1447-557X

National Library of Australia—Cataloguing-in-Publication Data:

Author:	Frost, Andrew.
Title:	The boys / Andrew Frost.
ISBN:	9780868198620 (pbk.)
Series:	Australian screen classics.
Notes:	Bibliography.
Subjects:	Graham, Gordon, 1949– The boys.
	Graham, Gordon, 1949—Film and video adaptations.
	The boys (Motion picture).
	Feature films—Australia—History and criticism.
Dewey Number:	791.4372

Cover design by Emma Vine, Currency Press

Front cover shows David Wenham.

Typeset by Currency Press in Iowan Old Style roman 9.5 pt.

Printed by Hyde Park Press, Richmond, SA

All photographs within the text are from *The Boys,* © Arena Films

AUSTRALIAN SCREEN CLASSICS

JANE MILLS
Series Editor

Our national cinema plays a vital role in our cultural heritage and in showing us at least something of what it is to be Australian. But the picture can get blurred by unruly forces such as competing artistic aims, inconstant personal tastes, political vagaries, constantly changing priorities in screen education and training, technological innovation and market forces.

When these forces remain unconnected, the result can be an artistically impoverished cinema and audiences who are disinclined to seek out and derive pleasure from a diverse range of films, including Australian ones.

This series is a part of screen culture which is the glue needed to stick these forces together. It's the plankton in the moving image food chain that feeds the imagination of our filmmakers and their audiences. It's what makes sense of the opinions, memories, responses, knowledge and exchange of ideas about film.

Above all, screen culture is informed by a *love* of cinema. And it has to be carefully nurtured if we are to understand and appreciate the aesthetic, moral, intellectual and sentient value of our national cinema.

Australian Screen Classics will match some of our best-loved films with some of our most distinguished writers and thinkers, drawn from the worlds of culture, criticism and politics. All we ask of our writers is that they feel passionate about the films they choose. Through these thoughtful, elegantly-written books, we hope that screen culture will work its sticky magic and introduce more audiences to Australian cinema.

Jane Mills is Associate Professor in Communication in the School of Communication and Creative Industries at Charles Sturt University, Associate Senior Research Fellow at the Australian Film, Television & Radio School, and a member of the Board of Directors of the Sydney Film Festival. Her most recent book is Loving and Hating Hollywood: Reframing Global and Local Cinemas.

CONTENTS

ACKNOWLEDGEMENTS

Thanks must first go to my editor Jane Mills for her forensic attention to detail; her many, many helpful suggestions, for her good humour and seemingly limitless patience.

Thanks also to Carrie Miller for suggesting my name in the first place. The series editor would also like to add her thanks to mine. I'd also like to thank her for her enthusiastic support and good friendship.

A huge debt of gratitude is owed to Rowan Woods for his generosity and time—and for helping me to remember events in their proper order.

Thanks should also go to Arena Films and to all at Currency Press.

Andrew Frost

INTRODUCTION

This is a book about a movie; it's about a place and a time that led up to the making of *The Boys*. This is also a story about how the themes of the film, its ideas and approaches fit into a broader context of Australian filmmaking. It became impossible to tell this story without talking about my own peripheral relationship to the film, insofar as I knew a few of the people involved in its making, but also it was necessary to acknowledge the emotional connection I feel towards *The Boys* as an exemplary Australian movie. The structure of this book is fragmented, following the byways of memory and recollection, focusing on the film and its themes and ideas. It's my hope that this approach is faithful to its creative spirit. For those who want to jump straight into the movie, go to Chapter 2. For those who want to know the full story, let's start here…

Brett Sprague (David Wenham).

I

FLASH FORWARD

Brett Sprague, a man in his early thirties perhaps, is talking to his younger brothers, Stevie and Glenn. They sit in Stevie's childhood bedroom—clouds-on-blue-sky wallpaper, toy cars lined up on bookshelves, old paperbacks nestled together, covers curled and filthy. Brett's face is a pallid frame for cold eyes that regard his brothers with calculated detachment. Something inside him has soured, but now it is time to act—to regain to his pride and his manhood. They arm themselves with a sharpened screwdriver. It's time to leave. The brothers no longer resist. Brett is in control. It is, as he will soon say, as God himself planned it...

Anita and Beyond

I was turning 24. It was a Saturday—1 March 1986. What to do to celebrate? All my close friends, even my girlfriend, were out of town. But there was still hope for a big night. My friend Catherine was organising a party for me. 'Just come around to my place at 7pm', she'd said a few days before, 'it'll be great!' Her enthusiasm was always infectious. Catherine was someone who made you feel as though you were part of her gang, a bunch of bad kids who'd no doubt smoked at the back of the school bus, but who were now semi-grown up artists and dancers and filmmakers and would-be poet-philosophers. To have a party with Catherine was to have a great time. I was set.

But what to do with the rest of the day? I always get caught by indecision when I have nothing planned—I stared out the window and watched the clouds. I decided to go out for the day to Paddington Markets in Sydney's eastern suburbs—a groovy-fashion-designer-bargains-cheap-records-and-paperbacks-type thing that ran every Saturday. My plan was to catch the bus from Glebe, across the inner city to Paddington, and visit friends who sold their homemade t-shirts from a stall; I'd spend most of the afternoon with Mary and Romana.

I sat in the market watching the shoppers come and go. We ate hot chips and eventually, inevitably perhaps, our discussion turned to the recent murder of Anita Cobby. The details of the crime were slowly coming out in the press and they were horrifying. She was a nurse who had been waiting at a bus stop outside a train station. Somehow she'd been wrestled into a car, taken to a field, raped, and then…

The thought of it was too horrible to hold in the mind. Mary and Romana didn't want to talk about it much. I decided it was probably time to go home. After saying farewell I caught a cab back home to Glebe. The cab driver was listening to the news on the radio and again the conversation turned to Cobby. The cab driver said that five guys were being held, three of them brothers, and they'd 'fucking cut her up mate, bit by bit'. The driver was appalled. He wanted them dead.

At home I showered and changed for the birthday party, gelled my hair, put on my heavy dark overcoat—standard inner-city issue of the day—and took a cab to Surry Hills, arriving at Catherine's right on 7pm. I knocked. Nothing. I knocked again. The door opened and Catherine was in a towel. She was annoyed I'd made her come to the front door from the shower. 'What?' she asked.

Catherine had completely forgotten about her promise of a party. She invited me in, gave me a glass of red wine and ushered me into the living room. She went upstairs to get dressed. I sat alone until her flatmate, Graham, arrived home with Udo, a Finnish sailor he'd just picked up in Hyde Park. Graham put on a record—Cabaret Voltaire's *Red Mecca*—as Udo clunked his biker boots down on the coffee table. In the kitchen for a refill of wine, Graham told me that Udo had approached him in the War Memorial, suggesting it might be possible to defecate near the Tomb of the Unknown Soldier, and that no-one would know.

Catherine eventually returned to the living room wearing her black leather biker jacket, leather skirt, knee high boots and fishnet stockings. She stood at the mirror in the lounge room touching up her makeup and fussing over her bleached blonde hair. Udo and Graham sat silently staring at me. Catherine announced that she was going out to dinner with her friends and, as a consolation for the forgotten party, I could come along.

The restaurant was just around the corner. As we walked down the street, her high heels clicking on the concrete, Catherine strongly advised me—*insisted*—that it was probably best if I didn't talk about Cobby at dinner. We were going to meet a group of women that Catherine had first met while she was doing Fine Arts at Sydney Uni. They were hardcore new wave feminists and they wouldn't tolerate my bullshit. I'd met some of those women before and I was a little afraid, a little in awe, and so I agreed that I wouldn't say anything.

The entrées might have arrived by the time the subject of Cobby came up, but it didn't take long, and thankfully it wasn't me who'd mentioned it. Catherine glared at me from across the table anyway but I just shrugged. I was the only male at the table of seven, and although the women didn't hold me personally responsible for the murder, I certainly felt complicit. I argued that even if the death penalty *could* be specially reintroduced for the murderers it might be prudent to have a trial first, *and then* hang them. The opposing views were divergent and vigorously argued. Patriarchy and misogyny were the root cause, with phallocentric capitalism aiding and abetting. The volume of the conversation grew louder. The owner of the restaurant came over and asked us to keep it down. The argument—and the meal—ended in a tense silence.

The restaurant was nearly empty by the time we left. Catherine grabbed my arm as we stepped out on to Crown Street and took me to the Taxi Club, a late night drinking venue for taxi drivers, their friends and 'guests'—meaning a lot of Tongan and Fijian transvestites and their boyfriends, straight looking, Westie guys in flannel shirts and jeans who played the club's poker machines. The first floor bar sold hot food that slowly baked in bains-marie under squalid yellow lights. The room glowed like a sickly 3am sunset.

Catherine surveyed the motley crowd and said, 'Fuck art, let's dance'. On the way up the carpeted stairs to the disco we were blocked by square-headed bouncers who held back the crowd. Two other uniformed guys were beating a man's face to a bloody mess. We quickly retreated downstairs. We found John L. and Kristina at the bar. We drank more beer. Kristina said she'd read that Anita Cobby was a nurse and was a beauty queen when she was younger. Time passed as I beat the sober feeling of dinner into submission. John L. gave me a lift home.[1] On the way out to the car we saw the man beaten by the bouncers hanging on to a pole, the man's girlfriend tearfully urging him to call the police, the man, his face contorted and swollen, saying repeatedly, 'Nah, it's not worth it, *it's just not worth it...* '

I awoke with a blistering hangover. My sister called and asked if I'd like to go for a drive in the country and receive a belated birthday present. The only problem was I'd have to catch a train out to the 'burbs. Sue was house-sitting my father's place way out in the north-western suburbs while he was away on holiday. Sure, I said, and slowly got myself together, showered, and dressed. Just before I left the house Catherine rang to apologise for the terrible night out and the verbal savaging I'd received at dinner. We both laughed. Yeah, it had been full on. She promised she'd take me out again, only we'd do things properly the next time.

We—me, Sean and Nick and Rowan—were supposed to be making a new movie and I had intended on writing some ideas down in my notebook during the long train journey along the Epping line. But I couldn't concentrate. I was too hung-over, and a family of four—two daughters, a mother and father—sitting in the seats next to me were talking about how Anita Cobby had been such a nice girl, and how horrible it must be for her parents.

I looked out the window and tried not to be sick. The only event that had been as big as this—an event that had dominated everything from the newspapers and television and talk-back radio to everyday people talking on the streets—had been the disappearance of a baby named Azaria Chamberlain at Uluru in 1980. The murder of Anita Cobby was something no-one seemed to be able to understand except in the same sort of Biblical terms—revenge, justice. Blood.

The train rocked slowly as it climbed a cutting outside Strathfield Station.

Exceptional Moments

As I was growing up in the suburbs of Sydney in the 1960s and '70 my favourite type of movies—genre is an unknown term when you're a kid—were war films and science fiction. I would search for those incredible moments of organised violence in stories set in World War II, or for those transcendent moments in SF when the very rules of space and time are distorted with spectacular special effects.

Drama requires that something happens, producing a pivotal moment when things change and people react. The exceptional moment, or set of circumstances are the core of drama. That's the basis of a story. Over the years, as my tastes became a little less detailed in their requirements, I was drawn to movies set in what could be loosely termed the 'real world'. But stories set in the real world, the recognisable one that seems more like day-to-day life, are themselves abstractions. I think of movies where 'nothing' happens—films like Andy Warhol's *Sleep* (1963) or *Empire* (1964), films that run for hours and present just one thing, slowly changing—and know that these are not *dramas* in the classic sense. They're thought experiments with a very particular aesthetic. What the mainstream audience is looking for are stories elegant in their structure, emotionally satisfying, and which provide a diverting entertainment. That's what a drama is, and to a large extent, it's the definition of what it is when we talk about a 'film'.

During my post-teenage years I thought that my tastes had 'developed'. I knew what genres were. Among my friends there were cults around certain movies, films like the hallucinatory multiple-identity-gangster-flick masterpiece *Performance* (Donald Cammell, 1970), the Vietnam war-bad-acid-trip-cum-road-movie *Apocalypse Now* (Francis Ford Coppola, 1979) or the extremely violent, ironically hilarious cocaine-80s version of *Scarface* (Brian De Palma, 1983). I could have quoted you whole swathes of dialogue from these movies and I thrilled to be part of the communal celebration of stories where men went beyond the limits of the acceptable, to act boldly, and bloodily, in demanding situations.[2] This was a different order of drama, still exceptional, but somehow more plausible in my mind.

I don't think it ever occurred to me then that I had simply shifted my pre-pubescent set of entertainment values to a different type of movie. My friends were all male, all 'boys' in the sense that we liked to get together, smoke pot and watch these films over and over, discuss them endlessly and when, at parties or on the street, or chatting on the phone, we'd drop into a line of dialogue from one of these films and use these exceptional stories as ironic counterpoints to our own very dull and standard lives. Yet I did know that I was bonding with my male friends through these absurdly inflated versions of masculinity, that while socially abhorrent—killers, soldiers, murderers and drug dealers—there were within these archetypes a tantalising hint of wish fulfilment.

Preview

It was a Tuesday morning in Sydney in early-1998—overcast, humid—and I was at an early morning preview screening of *The Boys*. The event had been hastily organised so that Australian film critics could see it before its official premiere at the Berlin Film Festival. After some perfunctory welcomes from the director, Rowan Woods, and the film's producer, Robert Connolly, the lights went down, and the movie began.

It's odd recalling how one felt after seeing a film for the first time. Most leave you with nothing but the occasional film is so remarkably different that even as you're watching it you know that it's something special. I recall sitting in a cinema and, at about the three quarter mark of Martin Scorsese's *Goodfellas* (1990), I was thinking, 'this is a masterpiece'. I had the same sensation during Paul Thomas Anderson's *There Will Be Blood* (2007). These films transcend the medium, their emotive power seems to eliminate the distance between the viewer and the subject on the screen and, while the emotions are fully engaged, there's a reflexive acknowledgement that a story is being told, that risks are being taken with the form of film itself, all feeding back into the full experience of the movie. This was happening in *The Boys*. I felt as though I couldn't breathe—the tension of the film was unrelenting.

Afterwards on the street outside the cinema with the screech of Sydney's comical monorail grinding overhead, I wandered in a daze back to work, knowing that I had just seen something amazing. Sitting at my computer in the office I wasn't really working—I was lost in the memory of *The Boys*, sifting through its parts, piecing together in my mind its boldly fractured narrative structure, considering its stunning performances, the dark humour that appeared at odd moments, and trying to come to terms with the fact that someone I knew had directed a debut feature that was easily one of the best, if not *the* best, Australian film ever made.

I hadn't spoken to Rowan in years. We'd met at City Art Institute in the early 1980s and we'd become friends.[3] Rowan hooked up with Nick Meyers and Sean O'Brien, old friends of mine who I'd first met in the '70s.[4] We'd all been very close. We collaborated on films and hatched grand plans to make masterpieces and luxuriate in the fame and wealth enjoyed by superstar directors. It had all come to nothing—or at least well short of my short-term ambitions—and we slowly drifted apart, disappointed, and although Rowan and I were never on bad terms, his distance was still painful.

Seeing *The Boys* put all that personal history aside. I knew that what I wanted to do was to pick up the phone and congratulate him. I tracked down his mobile number and called him the moment I arrived home from work. The film is great I said, it's incredible, a masterpiece. Rowan was suitably modest but he was proud of it. And so was I. It felt as though he had scored goal for the home team, one for the true believers—for those who had travelled together.

Australian Movies

It was probably around 1974 and I was on holidays with my cousins in the small rural town of Moree in north-western New South Wales. The backs of my thighs were stuck to the clammy surface of the vinyl leather-look couch in Uncle Neville's lounge room. A potted plant stood next to a faux-wooden sideboard arranged with his various awards for service from the local council and a decanter of sherry with its matching but incomplete set of glasses. There was a single armchair, a coffee table, a framed picture of a beach scene on the wall and an empty magazine rack.

And there was a black and white television set playing scenes from a nightmare.

A blonde-haired, effete school teacher named John Grant is on a kangaroo cull with a bunch of sweat-stained ockers, blazing through the night in a battered convertible, a spotlight on top and guns firing. They're mowing down every living thing in their path. Kangaroos caught in the headlights are shot, dismembered—and left to putrefy in the desert sun. Massive quantities of beer are drunk. Grant attempts to have drunken sex with a woman, but the need to vomit interrupts the act. The sun sets over the desert. Grant attempts to leave the town by hitchhiking on a truck. And he ends up back where he started. Grant's intention was to go on a holiday. Instead, he finds himself in a landscape of such unrelenting and unforgiving horror that, in the end, the only option seems to be suicide. When even that fails, he catches a train back to his school.

The film was *Wake in Fright* (1971).[5] John Grant—played by British actor Gary Bond—was trying to escape an outback Australian town that, in its general features of town hall, main street, pubs and people, looked disturbingly like Moree.[6] The town in *Wake in Fright* was full of Aussie grotesques, from Chips Rafferty's hard drinking policeman to the always more than slightly perverse British actor Donald Pleasence's alcoholic doctor, gone to seed, living alone in a tin shack. The film evoked a familiar landscape, one just like my cousin's outback home, but one that had been heightened into a feverish vision. Although *Wake in Fright* had been directed by the Canadian Ted Kotcheff, the film's lurid intensity seemed to me, even at the age of 12, to be a spiritually faithful version of the culture I was living in. And it was ironically appropriate that it would be played on a regional

TV station whose logo was an Aboriginal guy with a spear hunting down a kangaroo, both silhouetted against a livid, setting sun.

It wasn't the first Australian film I'd ever seen—I'd watched *Smiley Gets A Gun* (Anthony Kimmins, 1958) and *40,000 Horsemen* (Charles Chauvel, 1940) at school—but this is my earliest memory of consciously seeing an *Australian* film. More than that, *Wake in Fright* was the first film set in Australia to have a lasting effect on me.

My family's rare trips to the cinema or to the drive-in were to see the latest Disney films, quaint English comedies and later, when we were older, big budget American crime and action movies. Television was the place where you saw things that looked like home, a place where the stories were modest, downbeat and sincere. I remember hard-working Melbourne cops doing their jobs, old and friendly newsreaders in suits and black ties, funny men with rubbery faces on variety shows who made my dad laugh.

By the mid-1970s television had become a great educator in contemporary cinema. You could discover which of the Hollywood studios were making the most interesting movies and recognise their logos. If I saw the mountain peak and stars of Paramount, it might be a political thriller like *Three Days of the Condor* (Sydney Pollack, 1975) while the shield and clouds of Warner Bros. might herald the beginning of a *Dirty Harry* (Don Siegel, 1971) or better yet, a science fiction movie such as *THX 1138* (George Lucas, 1971). Late night TV time slots held the wonders of films by Robert Altman, Hal Ashby and Mike Nichols, the trash and treasure of B-Movies from American International Pictures and assorted ancient examples of British social realism.

The renaissance of Australian filmmaking in the 1970s that was dubbed 'New Wave' had leapt out of the cinemas. Many of the 'quality' examples of the new wave like Ken Hannam's outback sheep-shearer classic *Sunday Too Far Away* (1975), Fred Schepisi's haunting revelation of repressed homosexuality in a boy's Roman Catholic school in *The Devil's Playground* (1976) and Bruce Beresford's sadly funny tale of middle-class Labour voters in *Don's Party* (1976), were all screened on commercial television. Happily the sensation that was *Alvin Purple* (Tim Burstall, 1973) and its equally sex-obsessed sequel, *Alvin Rides Again* (David Bilcock and Robin Copping, 1974)—both a frustrating mystery to me due to their adult-only cinema ratings—gave birth to a raunchy TV series in 1976 of which I was an avid viewer. Along with sex comedies and the ribald humour of Beresford's *The Adventures of Barry McKenzie* (1972) and its sequel, *Barry McKenzie Holds his Own* (1974) the self-consciously middle-brow drama of movies like the mystery-horror films, *Summerfield* (Ken Hannam, 1977) and *Long Weekend* (Colin Eggleston, 1978) made up a heady mix of TV programming.[7]

Thinking back on this period it is remarkable how everything seemed to just *go together* as a matter of course. I vividly recall going to see Nicolas Roeg's *The Man Who Fell to Earth* (1976) at my local cinema in 1977. As a teenager with obsessive interests in science fiction and music, anything with David Bowie as an alien would have had me lining up for a ticket. This R-rated, mid-70s classic was given a brutal pruning for its Australian release to achieve a more audience-friendly M-certificate that would allow under-18s into the cinema. And so I went with a couple of friends one Saturday afternoon only to find that it was the second part of a double-bill with an unknown Australian film by first time director, Mike Thornhill, called *The F.J. Holden* (1977).

My friends—sci-fi purists and teenage prudes—were aghast.

The F.J. Holden was a story of a suburban bloke named Kev (Paul Couzens), his girlfriend Anne (Eva Dickinson), his best mate Bob (Carl Stever) and the car of the title. Little of the plot remains in my memory, except for a lot of frank on-screen sex, drinking and driving around in the titular car. I felt instinctively that the acting was poor and the direction rudimentary, but the movie did look and feel like the world I lived in. I recall one scene: after a night out with his mates Kev lays in bed the next morning with a hangover. Kev's dad mows the lawn right outside his bedroom window, the mind-numbing rumble of the mower a none-too-subtle reminder that suburban life goes on. The hot red bricks of the house looked like the street I grew up in and the actor playing Kev's father had the same potato Irish features as my uncles. And I liked the on-screen sex. That was good. It all seemed very real. Then David Bowie appeared at the top of a hill in the opening scenes of the next film on the bill, stumbling down in the dust to a river where he carefully cupped water in his hands, drank, and then counted out a wad of cash. The alien had arrived.

This bizarre collision wasn't anything out of the ordinary. As my interest in the movies evolved I found myself seeking out screenings of obscure titles like the surrealist French-Czech animated sci-fi parable, *La planète sauvage* (*Fantastic Planet*) (René Laloux, 1973), or David Lynch's *Eraserhead* (1977). In the pre-video era seeing movies at repertory art-house cinemas was the only way you could get to see films that had long since passed from first release or were marketed as too 'weird' for mainstream audiences. The double-bill was standard fare.[8] I wonder who it was who thought that the pairing of Robert Altman's rambling music-and-politics classic *Nashville* (1975) with the ancient black-and-white horror movie, *Freaks* (Tod Browning, 1932) was great programming, yet there they were, a perennial double bill that screened at Dave's Encore Cinema at the Roma on Sydney's George Street for what felt like a decade.

This eclectic free-for-all on TV and at the movies created a profound sense of dissociation when it came to the concept of cinematic purism. The high culture end of Australian cinema—typified by tiresome faux European-style movies like Peter Weir's *Picnic at Hanging Rock* (1975) or Gillian Armstrong's *My Brilliant Career* (1979)—the kinds of movies celebrated as 'quality'—seemed to me to be distant and removed from real life. Out in the suburbs it was all weird aliens, back-seat sex romps and pop music fantasies.

The Super '80s

The 1980s were a kind of sunny headache. Every day you woke up to someone telling you how amazing everything was. It was the decade of the year of the book, it was the future, and it was everywhere. It was a time before DVDs and VHS, an age when most TV stations went dead at midnight. It was as though the '70s didn't really end until about 1984 when the headline stuff of news montages begins to kick in—Ronald Reagan, Thatcher's Britain™, and *Crocodile Dundee* (Peter Faiman, 1986)—but it finally comes into focus as I recall the era known as 'The Super '80s.'[9]

I started the decade in art school studying film, video and conceptual art. The film scene outside college seemed pretty much dead. The New Wave of Australian cinema had come to an end as its star directors left for Hollywood or struggled to find support and audiences for projects at home. A few notable features got made—George Miller's *Mad Max 2* (1981) or Ken Cameron's *Monkey Grip* (1982)—but in general the early part of the decade was a very dry season indeed. The alternative experimental cinema community that had formed around the Sydney Filmmakers' Co-operative in the late '60s and '70s—and which had produced some incredibly adventurous films—was running out of energy too.

By contrast, Sydney's student-boho scene in the early part of the decade was thriving. Much of it was centred on the inner urban squats, warehouses and student households of Surry Hills, Darlinghurst, Kings Cross, Woolloomooloo and Newtown. If you were into music, you were probably into art-house movies too, and fanzine publishing, art galleries, cool bookshops, cafes, cinemas and the whole do-it-yourself philosophy of the Punk era. And a big part of this time was something called 'the super 8 scene'.

Super 8 was the epitome of DIY. Developed as a home movie medium in 1965, Super 8 was supported by a number of film stock and equipment manufacturers and, although the gauge had a number of significant technical limitations, it was widely available and relatively cheap.[10] The expense of 16mm production was prohibitive and the screening of video was restricted to the number of people you could crowd around a monitor. About the only viable option was Super 8. With this ageing consumer technology in hand, filmmakers could seek to emulate mainstream cinema with sophisticated and semi-professional productions utilising actors, lighting and complex post-production. Or they could just as easily shoot off a roll of film and screen the raw results.

This odd mixture of circumstances led to the creation in 1983 of the Sydney Super 8 Film Group, a group of about ten or so people who organised film screenings, film festivals, the publication of readers and magazines and who vigorously proselytized the cause of Super 8 independent film making.[11] I joined the group in 1983 and hung around until 1988, running the group's office upstairs in a dusty and impossible-to-clean office on busy William Street, helping to choose films for screenings and making my own movies.

In the absence of anything else—and this was long before the advent of the short film festivals like TropFest and all the other festivals that arose in its wake[12]—the Sydney Super 8 Film Festivals were the place to see the thousands of short films being made by students, serious would-be filmmakers, dilettante scenesters and people who just wanted to have a go.

The basic film education that I'd picked up from watching TV and going to art-house cinemas wasn't unique by any means, in fact, it was a generational rite of passage to have stayed up late enough, and stayed awake long enough, to have watched Arthur Penn's *Mickey One* (1965) on TV, or gone to the movies at Sydney University's Footbridge Theatre to see Jean-Luc Godard's *One Plus One* (1968), to have trekked over to the Valhalla Cinema in Glebe to see Scorsese's *Mean Streets* (1973), or caught US avant-garde filmmakers Maya Deren and Alexander Hammid's poetic-experimental classic, *Meshes of the Afternoon* (1943), and Nicholas Ray's hysterical-camp masterpiece, *Johnny Guitar* (1954), in the art school's film history course. The eclecticism of the '70s seemed to speed up in the early 1980s.

In 1982 at a screening of student films at the art college I saw an ambitious video called *Reaction Football* directed by Rowan Woods. It was a mixture of documentary street reportage and a poetic-narrative essay film featuring interviews with fans of the Balmain Tigers rugby league team and underwater sequences of tropical fish. A voice over explained that the filmmaker was searching for the connection 'between fish and football'.

Reaction Football was different to anything anyone else had made. Student art films were more interested in poetic lyricism or performance art documentation than they were in constructing a narrative—or having a sense of humour. The ambition of Rowan's video was impressive too. I had to meet the guy who had made it.

Rowan was a recognisable figure around campus. Tall and slender, with a mad crop of orange hair, he wore unfashionable white jeans and football shirts. He was slightly older than most of the other students in the year, having spent a couple of semesters at Sydney University studying marine biology and acting in Sydney University Dramatic Society productions. Dropping out of university he wound up at City Art Institute. Rowan embraced everything about the suburban experience I was trying to leave behind—working-class culture like football, rock music of the '70s—all the stuff you were supposed to forget if you were cool and living in the inner city of Sydney in the early '80s.

Most of the films being screened at Super 8 festivals were self-consciously 'experimental' and the influence of the 'art school aesthetic' was enormous. Very few produced films that attempted a conventional narrative, or indeed, a story at all. My own collaborative efforts with Nick Meyers and Sean O'Brien were different because our shared interests in movies of the '70s—and narrative filmmaking in general—were at odds with the prevailing style.[13] Rowan was a natural addition to our small crew. Together we made a road movie, *Edge of Nowhere* (1985), a tribute to all the late night movies of our teens; *Ropo's Movie Nite* (1986) parodied both pro and amateur Aussie film-making culture (with dialogue purloined from Weir's *Picnic at Hanging Rock*); while our magnum opus *The Big Lunch* (1988), starred Rowan as an AWOL Naval officer, and featured more than 25 speaking parts.[14] Our swansong, *It's All True* (1988), was a six-part portmanteau film that included a fake confessional from Rowan recalling his filmmaking philosophy and his exploits as a marine biologist.[15]

Rowan's own filmmaking went ahead quickly. In 1984 he directed *Suspect Filmmaker*, a pointed comedic critique of Wim Wenders, the German director who was considered a demigod of European independent and art-house filmmaking. Wenders' 1982 film *The State of Things*—a semi-autobiographical film about a low budget filmmaker and his often inept crew—and his lost-in-exotic-locations documentary *Tokyo-Ga* (1985)—set new benchmarks for the vaulting pretension of anyone wanting to make cinematic art and transcend the inner city scene.[16] Collaborating with a friend from Sydney University drama days named Peter Alexiadis, Woods's *Suspect Filmmaker* was the sensation of the 1983 Sydney Super 8 Film Festival.[17] Along with its jokes and parody of Wenders, the film used professional filmmaking techniques—the film had a performance, it featured a tracking camera and a dolly. It had sound. It was a *real* movie.

The next couple of projects stepped out yet further into semi-professional territory. Woods attempted a short feature on 16mm called *Remind Me Tomorrow* that was never completed. In 1984, *Kenny's Love* was his graduation film from City Art Institute. Following the character of Kenny—played by Woods—the film is a character study of a mentally disabled man who makes his living by selling hot dogs outside rugby league games. For *Kenny's Love* Woods had returned to the football obsessions that had inspired *Reaction Football*. Shot on 16mm and edited by Nick Meyers, *Kenny's Love* was as ambitious as Woods's other student work and was a *homage* to Martin Scorsese's *Taxi Driver* (1976), transposing the madness of the Travis Bickle character into a forlorn yet naively optimistic character.

The short film's plot involves a visit from Kenny's sister who expresses concern that Kenny can't go on living as he does, alone in a one-bedroom flat, and will need care. Like Woods' subsequent feature films, family is a major theme of the story; Kenny's connection to it, and the estrangement from the 'normal' world that is embodied in his intellectual disability. Kenny's obsession with football gives him a connection to the normalising masculine world of football and its fans, but he is physically removed from it. As he slowly patrols the empty space of the stadium awaiting a customer, the roars of the crowd reverberate from concrete walls. Kenny is both a part of the world but distant to it. The roots of many of Woods's approaches to the language of film making, from editing and the placement of the camera to mise en scène and soundscape can be found in *Kenny's Love*.

In 1988, while recovering from the serious injuries he sustained in a car accident in 1986, Woods undertook a Master of Arts at City Art Institute. The Masters project began as a script for a feature film based on Sophocles' *Oedipus Rex* transposed into the world of rugby league clubs. Although the film script was completed the film itself was never made. As part of his Masters project, Woods also made a series of large-scale photographic prints that depicted scenes from the script, a mixture of quasi-classical poses shot in the St. George Leagues Club.[18] The resulting images were frankly ridiculous, yet compelling: the high drama of Greek Tragedy mixed with the pathos of bars, plush-wallpaper and meat trays.

A Band Apart

Making movies with Nick and Sean, Rowan, Catherine and Simon, was a bit like being a part of a gang—a geeky, self-aware group with its own in-jokes, sense of humour, points of reference and ambitions.[19] Our sense of identity was very much drawn as an idea in opposition to the prevailing industry of filmmaking—something called 'professionalism'—and a sense of solidarity among five 20-somethings who were yet to get their breaks.

The movies I've described here—the amateur efforts and the semi-pro productions—form a sort of prelude. With only the vaguest sense of nostalgia, I recall the Super '80s as a time of possibility. We spent endless hours discussing favourite movies, the nuances of their making, their intentions. Or we'd talk about dream projects. In my memory, everything we did was based around the streets of Surry Hills—walking up and down the night-time footpaths, the asphalt still hot from the summer sun—on our way to buy a bad take-away pizza on Crown Street, a few bottles of beer and then back to Nick's place to push the script for *The Big Lunch* along a few extra pages. It was great to be young.

Woods acted in a number of low-budget Australian films while he developed his own projects, and then went to film school. In 1992, while a student at the Australian Film and Television School, he directed the short film *Tran the Man* (1993).[20] Starring David Wenham as Raymond 'Tran' Moss, Woods played the part of a heavy alongside the outstanding but under-used Australian actors Skye Wansey and Stephen Leeder. Elements of the film's plot and its mix of crime and social setting would later form the basis of Wood's second feature *Little Fish* (2005).[21]

In these years before he made *The Boys*, Woods pursued the goal of directing his own feature; *Tran the Man* was an important step in that progress. So too, perhaps, the episodes of *Police Rescue* he directed for TV in 1996 and episodes of teen soap *Heartbreak High* (1994). As the '80s turned into the '90s, the audiences that had come out for the Super 8 Film Festivals began to drop away and the scene that had supported the films and filmmakers of the Super '80s was over, the audience drawn to newer things, no longer interested in the little gauge that could. The few filmmakers who'd been seriously interested in making mainstream movies were starting to gain small footholds in the proper, grown-up industry...

Michelle (Toni Collette).

2

PRESS PLAY

There is a story—and then there is the telling of a story. Many films opt for a linear structure that places one event after the next leading to an often predictable conclusion. *The Boys* takes a different path. The audience must decipher the film's fragmented narrative as scenes that reveal what is to come occur out of strict chronological order. The full meaning of these scenes is only revealed at the end when the audience can then piece together what has happened, mentally reordering the events into a flow that makes sense when the full impact of the revelations become clear. The film is also notable for the fact that it is a story told in detail—its drama is centred on the interactions of its characters, in their looks and glances, in the meeting of eyes and the avoidance of stares. The dialogue of the film is often assaultive and confronting. Yet at other times it is elliptical and unresolved—when something is being said, other things are meant. To tell the story of the film is therefore to relate its micronarrative and texture, its minutely observed interactions, and to describe its approach to looking—and seeing.

The Boys denies one of the central conventions of cinema—the ability to see what is happening. From the very outset elements of the action are shrouded in darkness. After the moody opening night sequence with its dark roads and whiteouts, we first see Brett Sprague (David Wenham) as he is released from prison. He is a silhouette set against the distant gates and fences of the jail—as the door of the inner prison lockup is raised he is revealed as a black figure devoid of detail, perhaps implying that Brett is already beyond the reach of light. This oscillation between *seeing* and *not seeing* is the film's main visual theme.

The film is constructed as a series of parallel narrative spaces; there is the main action enclosed within the confines of the suburban house which is presented as *current time*; there are the *flash forwards* that reveal what is to come; and there is the eerie *other space* of the titles and those sequences throughout the film that suggest an estranged point of view.[22] Each of these narrative spaces has a distinct visual style—the other space is represented by the use of Hi 8 video refilmed from a video monitor, a process that highlights the pixilated grain of the TV picture, adding yet another visual layer between the audience and the action and suggesting that the notionally 'real' aspects of the image are at once, or twice, remove. The flash forwards have an unnerving stillness to them, and although the camera pans or the image cuts, the look of these sequences is remarkably different to the main body of the film. This look was achieved by simply placing the camera on a locked off tripod, whereas the rest of the film, the current time, with its uncertain, slightly shaky movements, was achieved by the director of photography Tristan Milani shooting the film off the shoulder.

These three filmic spaces will join at the end of the film as 'current time' catches up with the first of the flash forwards—approximately 18 hours after the action at the beginning of the film.

Opening Credits

The film begins with the nagging insistence of a bad dream. The music by The Necks pulses into menacing life—drum beats; a repeating sequence of acoustic bass notes; a droning electronic undercurrent and, floating over the top, unresolved piano chords. Awash in a pixilated blur, the camera tracks over people in shops at night, an amplified voice echoes, a series of announcements, perhaps from a nearby train station. The images dissolve into the next sequence; building lights, small dots of white amid the visual noise of video tape, the camera advancing forward, the images as seen from a car, lights burning out the screen to white, car headlights, white lines on black tarmac—the main title—'the boys' appears in lower case, in a deep orange, 'the' in sharp focus—'boys', fuzzy and indistinct.[23]

The location changes to a sequence of close-up interior shots that shift focus from abstract shapes to uncertain reality: a TV set seen through a doorway from another room—the names of the film's actors appearing around the frame—a sudden pan picks up an empty clothes hanger; a pull focus on a drain with white matter clogging up the holes; a grubby fry pan, knives on the kitchen wall, a light switch greyed with fingerprints. It is the detritus of suburban life captured with the forensic detachment of crime scene photography. Despite this apparent objectivity, the shifts in focus and the sudden moves of the camera imply that all this is a *subjective* view. But whose point of view is this? What has happened? And what is about to happen? The static interior images shift again—a ceiling light, an air-conditioned mounted high on a wall.[24]

And so begins *The Boys*. The film introduces its characters, its conflicts and drama. Something bad has happened and something even worse is coming. You can feel it.

Introducing the boys

Brett Sprague, the oldest of three brothers, has been away in prison for twelve months. On the day of his release he is picked up at the prison gates by his youngest brother Stevie (Anthony Hayes). He waits by the side of the road, sullen, in old faded clothes, kicking dirt with his feet. Brett considers a single cigarette in a crushed packet... He carefully replaces it. Brett was jailed for the assault on Graham Newman (Peter Hehir), the publican of the Fife and Drum. Now he's out of prison, Brett's plan is to re-establish his authority in the family, resume his criminal enterprise selling drugs—and exact revenge on those who he strongly suspects betrayed him: his brothers. He will be reunited with his family: his mum, Sandra (Lynette Curran), his girlfriend, Michelle (Toni Collette), and Stevie's pregnant teenage girlfriend, Nola (Anna Lise). On the way home Stevie tells Brett that although the family never found the time to come and visit, they had often thought of him. Brett, disgusted, announces he was abandoned. Does Brett truly believe what Stevie is saying? Brett's manner is cold, distant, yet his anger is palpable. Has Stevie been hitting on his girlfriend as well? Brett asks. Stevie claims their brother Glenn (John Polson) has been trying it on with Michelle, not him.

At home, it's all smiles and kisses from mum. Standing coyly to one side, her dyed hair done up in careful curls and a ponytail, Michelle smiles too. 'You been keeping it warm for me?' Brett asks as they kiss. Soon Brett's younger brother, Glenn, and his wife, Jackie (Jeanette Cronin), arrive. It's a 'welcome home' from the extended family.

Back in his bedroom—decorated with fantasy sci-fi art posters and cut-outs of nudes sticky-taped to the back of the door—Brett finds that a hollowed out sci-fi paperback, *The Moons of Infinity*, that had once contained his drug stash is now empty. Worse, the cupboard in which it was kept was locked; someone has raided his supply and that someone had a key. But who? While Brett ponders these questions Michelle enters the room, showing him that her hair is tyed back with a scrunchie that Brett had once given her. She lies on his bed. As they kiss, Brett asks if she's been unfaithful to him. Although she denies it, Brett is sceptical: 'You had it locked up and threw away the key?' he asks.

Flash forward: EIGHTEEN HOURS LATER. Dressed only in his underwear, Brett is in the backyard burning his clothes. Sandra watches through the window. As Brett washes his hands at the kitchen sink, Sandra stares in disbelief. 'Don't believe

'She lies on his bed. They kiss.'

nothing you hear Mum', he says. 'It's all fucking bullshit.' As Brett steps outside again he is wrestled to the ground by police.

As the boys gather for a family photo, tensions simmer. Brett suddenly accuses Glenn of always having been a 'fucking liar'. As Glenn defends himself, Sandra interrupts before the argument can escalate. Wandering into the kitchen Nola innocently asks—'What were you inside for?' Brett answers calmly—assault with a deadly weapon, and grievous bodily harm. Although Brett had used a

Glenn (John Polson).

sharpened screwdriver in the attack, Newman, the publican, had used a carving knife to defend himself. Brett lifts his sweatshirt to reveal a long scar. 'Nearly lost his spleen', says Sandra, offering some justification for Brett's actions.

*

Sandra is visited by Nick (Sal Sharah), who has come to collect the piecework she produces to support the family. Their conversation is perfunctory. Nick leaves with boxes stacked high. 'I hope you realise how hard your mum works for you', he says to Brett.

Flash forward: TWO DAYS LATER. Glenn watches as a uniformed policeman approaches him—Glenn's face is somewhere between terror and hopeless resignation. He is brutally punched and kicked to the ground. Stevie and Glenn are led through the rain to waiting police cars. Brett's ghostly white face is seen in the blizzard of static on a closed circuit television—he is in solitary confinement...

The boys go out for beer. But there is a problem—no-one has any money. Glenn asks Jackie for some cash, and despite her demand that they leave so they can get to work, Glenn insists that he's having *just one beer* with his brothers and *then* he will leave. They head out in Stevie's car, Brett behind the wheel. At high speed, the car blasts through traffic, runs orange and red lights, Stevie and Glenn screaming to slow down. As the car rolls into the Fife and Drum bottle shop driveway, Graham Newman sees them arrive. He presses a silent alarm button—beneath the counter is a carving knife.

The encounter between the Sprague boys and Newman is bitter. Newman's offsider, Sparrow (Andrew Heys), appears and soon Stevie has to be pulled away from him. Newman plays it cool, laughing as Brett shows him the extensive scar he carries from the fight. 'Ooh, that must have hurt mate', Newman laughs. 'You know something Newman?' asks Brett, 'You'd look a whole lot better with your head hanging out your arse.' Newman just laughs, but Brett's tone suggests it's a threat he'd be happy to carry out.

As soon as the boys re-enter the Sprague house, Jackie pleads with Glenn to go to work. These attempts at reason are sidelined as Sandra unveils a sausage and salad lunch, served buffet-style. To humiliate his youngest brother by implying he is hen-pecked, Brett sarcastically tells Jackie that she has a nice car. Stung, Glenn interrupts to say that it was he who bought it. 'No', corrects Jackie, 'I paid for it.' Glenn insists that he bought the car. 'All you did was pay the deposit—and I'd like to know where you got the money for that.' Brett points out that the car is known as 'the big V'—the 'up yours' that Jackie has been giving the whole family. His accusations are sharp verbal jabs coated in sarcasm—but Glenn only looks on, despondent. Jackie returns the attack—'We felt a whole lot better off with you in prison' she says—before demanding that Glenn stand up for her. Glenn just shrugs. Jackie, in tears, leaves the room. Brett seems smugly satisfied with the emotional mayhem he is provoking.

In the bathroom, the boys talk, stubbies of beer in hand, as Stevie takes a piss. The shot takes in the whole cramped bathroom as Brett carefully shaves stray hairs from his face, Stevie at the toilet, Glenn against the wall. As the younger brothers jostle for space, the brothers knock into Brett. In a swift and dominating act Brett pushes Stevie's neck down, forcing his youngest brother to his hands and knees. The camera cuts in close to Brett, his lips close to Stevie's ear: 'You wouldn't last five seconds in jail. You'd be on the ground with your pants around your feet in no time.'

Moments later, a police car arrives at the house. Sandra answers the door. The police have received complaints from Newman that Brett was at the Fife and Drum making threats. Sandra denies that he was there, but coming up behind her with the air of a repentant child, his eyes wide and glassy, Brett admits he had been at the bottle shop. The police leave with a warning—stay away from Newman. As the police leave, Glenn sees that Jackie has driven away too—leaving him behind.

Flash forward: 3 WEEKS LATER. Sandra sits in the dim hallway of her house. The phone rings. She answers it without speaking, simply listening to a threatening male voice. 'Are you the mother of those fucking animals that killed that girl? You fucking slut... I know details of the case that the cops wouldn't give out... You fucking slut... ' Sandra does not speak, she does not move... Sandra's lover, Abo (Pete Smith), walks down the hallway, calmly takes the phone from her grasp, and hangs up.

As Stevie lights a cigarette near the front door, Brett confronts him, asking if he took the drugs. Stevie flatly denies knowing anything about it despite the fact that he and Nola had been sleeping in Brett's bedroom.

*

Lethargy creeps over the family post-lunch. We see a close up of Stevie's pallid face and puffy eyes as he watches TV, the meaningless chatter of a TV shopping channel filling the room. Michelle drifts around the house. In Brett's cramped bedroom Glenn complains about Jackie's departure while Brett offers advice—and is mocked by Michelle who listens from the hallway. In the kitchen, Sandra cleans up as Nola sits on a stool, her back to the camera, her face looking off. What is she doing? Perhaps watching TV—or just staring into nothing. Michelle enters, sits down on another stool and lights a cigarette. Sandra, busily cleaning, asks what the boys are up to. 'Whingeing', is Michelle's depressed reply. 'No matter how hard I try', says Sandra, 'it always ends up a bloody mess.'

Stevie (Anthony Hayes).

Nola, dressed in her track suit, baby pink jacket and carefully pinned and braided hair, suddenly turns to Michelle and Sandra and announces she wants to leave, to get away, and to go somewhere else. Michelle questions her. Where will she go? What money will she use? Nola doesn't know. Sandra calls Stevie into the room but he doesn't give a fuck—he doesn't believe that the child is his—she's been with many other men. Sandra asks Nola if any of this is true, and soon everyone is arguing. 'I just want to get away', says Nola, almost in tears.

Entering the kitchen, Brett asks 'What's wrong?' Michelle explains that Nola would rather spend a night in a bus station than spend another second in the house. Brett comforts Nola in the manner of an adult tending a child, hugging her close, but there is something deeply unsettling in his manner, as though this tenderness is a show, a cynical attempt to control her while performing his 'concern' for the rest of the family. 'That's what you should be doing', says Michelle, scolding Stevie—a point made with an outstretched finger and a lit cigarette. 'All I want to

Sandra (Lynette Currin).

do is get away', sobs Nola. 'Hey... no-one gets away', says Brett. 'You're one of us now.' It sounds more like a threat than words of comfort. 'You're carrying Mum's first grandchild.' When Brett tells Nola that he'd do anything to protect her, Stevie scoffs—'What the fuck are you talking about?' No-one seems to believe in Brett's show of concern, least of all Brett.

*

In Brett's bedroom, Michelle, who previously seemed to be supportive of Nola, blurts out: 'Just because she's having a kid doesn't make her family'. Brett stares into her eyes. 'I'd protect you as well.' Michelle just laughs. 'You must have been outta your head to do what you did.' Brett

'Just because she's having a kid doesn't make her family'.

looks away, seemingly uninterested in her opinion. 'You'll be heading straight back where you came from', she says. 'If I am then you'll miss the hard cock I've got saved up for you.' Michelle dismisses Brett. 'You haven't got it in you.' Michelle is the only one who can attest to Brett's virility and her denial of his power is either a challenge to it—or a mockery. Brett does not respond as Michelle leaves the room.

*

Later, back in the lounge room, Stevie entertains Brett and Glenn with an impression of a football commentator. It is a rare moment of humour. Suddenly Brett suggests that they all pay Newman another visit, but his brothers just laugh. After Newman's complaint to the cops, and their visit to the house, a return to the bottle shop would be insane. Brett lets the thought go. Stevie offers Brett a cigarette but he claims that he's given up. 'What's that in your pocket?' asks Stevie. Brett pulls out the cigarette from the battered packet that we saw at the beginning of the film. 'What this?' asks Brett. Stevie nods. 'That's me pride, mate.'

In the master bedroom, Sandra lies listlessly on her bed in her underwear, gently caressing a decorated hand fan with the tips of her fingers. Michelle enters slowly, her head appearing from behind the bedroom door. 'It was the only thing he ever gave me', Sandra says wistfully. 'They all said they loved me—but they left me. You shouldn't leave anything you love.' Michelle asks Sandra if she knows what's going on with the boys—but Sandra pretends not to know what she's talking about.

Nola listens to the conversation from the next door bathroom, a close up of her face cold and white against the blue tiles of the room.

Michelle and Sandra continue to talk. Sandra's approach is to dismiss any criticism of her boys. 'What are they going to do—let off a bomb?' she asks. 'There are worse things in this world than my boys.' Michelle contemptuously claims that Sandra is afraid of her own family. Suddenly Sandra becomes angry. 'You try living around here and keeping a lid on things around here. *You try*.'

Nola (Anna Lise).

Back in the lounge room, we finally learn the truth—Brett and his brothers had been selling heroin at the Fife. The problem was that Newman hadn't given them the 'green light' and, according to Brett, Stevie had given the game away by talking to too many people. Wise to the Sprague's dealing, Brett had been caught by Newman, knifed and left for dead. 'It wasn't a hold up, it was a fucking set up', says Brett.

Cutting back to Sandra's bedroom, when Michelle suggests that she chain up her sons, Sandra is incensed: 'They're not *fucking dogs*—but I'll tell you one thing—while they're under this roof they'll do as they're told.' Michelle gives Sandra a contemptuous, withering stare, as judgemental and hateful as anything Brett can conjure.

Perhaps emboldened by her confrontation with Michelle—or perhaps mindful of the truth in Michelle's words—Sandra attempts to create order in the lounge room where the boys are now playing football and listening to loud music. They crash around the room, the camera observing the action at a distance. Sandra's resolve disappears as the boys insist she dance. Powerless, Sandra is soon being twirled around, laughing. Michelle, watching this boisterous display, decides to leave—but just as she opens the front door, Brett stops her. 'Taking a leaf out of Jackie's book?' asks Brett. 'What the fuck did they do to you in there?' asks Michelle. 'Did they give you a fucking lobotomy or something?' Michelle storms back to the kitchen. 'You're just a fucking loser', she yells. Until this moment it had seemed that Michelle had been Brett's closest ally. Although she had been the only one to openly mock him or doubt his words, Michelle seems to have had some influence over Brett. Now, with his behaviour becoming more extreme, his emotions more illogical and cut off from her influence or reason, Michelle looks scared.

Brett is aroused by Michelle's defiance and, with a hypnotic stare, the camera cutting close to their faces, says they should 'do it'. To get away from the rest of the family in the cramped house, Michelle suggests they go to the laundry. They kiss as they stumble into the filthy room crowded with lawn mowers, a spear gun and other assorted junk; Michelle pulls her top down, leans back on the sink, and spreads her knees. But Brett needs a moment as he fumbles with a hand in his pants—a moment that seems to last forever.

'Brett needs a moment.'

'You can't do it, can you?' Michelle mocks. Realisation dawns: 'You took it up the arse, didn't you?' Brett grabs her throat and attempts to kiss her, but she struggles away from his mouth. 'I did fuck someone else', she says defiantly—and Brett erupts, bashing her head against the laundry's fibro wall which cracks from the impact. Michelle struggles to get away, lashes out at Brett, and makes for the door. But as she opens it, Brett grabs her from her behind and is about to impale Michelle's eye on a rusty nail in the wall. She grimaces, her face contorted with fear, 'Please not the face', she whispers. 'I knew you fucked someone', says Brett into her ear, 'I'd never touch you in a million years.' Michelle stops fighting. 'Well, you're never going to get the chance', she cries.

She struggles free, Brett's fist grasping the scrunchie and a tuft of her hair that he has pulled out with brute force. She staggers across the backyard.

Back inside, Nola and Sandra look on quietly as Brett re-enters the house. 'Where's Michelle?' asks Sandra. 'I think she had to go to the little girl's room', says Brett innocently but unconvincingly. Brett leaves the room and Nola immediately picks up the telephone

Flash forward: SIX MONTHS LATER. A phone call from prison— Brett asks Sandra to bring Michelle to the prison so that he can sort out an alibi. But Sandra explains that Michelle isn't coming—she won't speak to anyone in the family. Brett insists she try. In an abrupt cut to outside a bleak suburban apartment, Sandra slowly climbs a set of stairs on the outside of a block of flats. Sandra pleads with Michelle through the keyhole of the closed front door. But Michelle stands inside, silent—unmoved.

'Where's Michelle?'

*

In the lounge room, the boys continue to drink. The atmosphere is tense and soon the conversation degenerates into a mindless argument—Brett claiming that Glenn's poorly paid job is exploitation, and since Jackie was the one who got him the job, she's exploiting him too. It's a cynical argument that Glenn does his best to reject—Jackie is the best thing that ever happened to him, he says. Stevie laughs derisively. Glenn says that,

'You fucking do what they're trying to do—but you fucking do it to them...'

instead of following Brett's example of going to jail, he and Jackie have *plans*—there is a choice to work hard and do good. 'No-one has a choice', counters Brett. Stevie offers his opinion—the world outside is like *Invasion of the Body Snatchers*—and like the aliens-in-human-form in the science fiction movie, all those in the outside world have to be destroyed—'Kill 'em with pitch forks'. 'No mate', says Brett. 'You fucking do what they're trying to do—but you fucking *do it to them...* '

A knock at the front door reveals the police. Reports of a woman screaming had been made by neighbours. Brett, cocky and confident that the police can't enter the house without permission or a warrant, mocks the officers. The police sense that Sandra is worried, but she remains silent, and they leave.

In the lounge room Sandra asks where Michelle is. They don't know. At the end of her tether, Sandra demands that the boys do something, *anything*, to escape their drunken lethargy. 'Get out of the house!', she screams. The boys are unmoved. Sandra asks Brett once again about Michelle, and when he denies knowing anything, she calls him a liar. Sandra tells her sons that they bring their misery on themselves—it's no wonder the police come around. Stevie reacts with a resentment that has no doubt been building for years—they are three brothers by two fathers—and who is Abo the father of? Stevie's claim is that one of the brothers has been fathered by Abo—an insult that Brett and Glenn react angrily to, and which denigrates Sandra for her relationship with a black man. The racist slur is rejected by Sandra who leaves the room in tears.

A phone call summons Glenn outside and into Jackie's car. She has returned—her lips trembling, her eyes wet, on the verge of tears—to offer one last chance to save their relationship; leave the brothers, don't see the family—it's them or me, says Jackie. Glenn cannot make the choice—so Jackie makes it for him. She throws her wedding ring at Glenn and leaves him to stagger back inside. In his bedroom, Brett finds Nola packing her belongings. She says she's just doing some laundry, but it is an obvious lie. Brett asks—why did she call the police on him? Nola, terrified, denies it, then under pressure—admits it. Brett tells her it's okay: 'Everyone makes mistakes sometimes'. Brett kisses Nola gently on the forehead.

*

In a return to the same eerie filmic *other space* of the opening titles we see a train station at night—the camera tracks along the lights and wires and gantry above the rail line. A cold voice echoes...

*

Brett re-enters his bedroom to finds that Nola has gone and taken all her clothes. Another of the women has made her escape.

*

Brett and Glenn talk in the lounge room. Glenn calls Jackie a 'fucking slut', over and over, a mantra of drunken despair.

*

When Stevie discovers that Nola has gone, he flips out, calling her a 'fucking bitch'. Staggering into the kitchen he demands that Sandra tell him where Nola is. The boys follow Stevie into the room. Sandra sees that Brett has Michelle's scrunchie in his back pocket and, now convinced he's hurt her, attacks him, pulling his hair. As Brett starts to fight back, Abo enters the kitchen to defend Sandra and separate them. He makes the mistake of telling Brett to fuck off and is bashed to the ground by Brett, and kicked and punched by Stevie. 'All I want is a bit of fucking respect in me own home', declares Brett. 'Is that too much to fucking ask?'

Flash Forward: ONE DAY BEFORE TRIAL. Sandra visits Brett in prison. She has a letter from Michelle that will explain why she won't come to his aid. Brett refuses to read it realising he has no hope. Sandra, in tears, explains that 'no-one is coming'. Brett dismisses her, his contempt disguised as concern. 'It must be very lonely', says Sandra. 'Sitting up there, looking down on the rest of us.'

In Stevie's childhood bedroom—now abandoned as a place to sleep with a partly dismantled car engine on the bed but still decorated with nursery wallpaper and toy cars—Brett decides that Graham Newman needs a 'taste of his own medicine'. Stevie offers futile alternatives—travelling north to Queensland, financing their trip with crime. Brett picks up a sharpened screwdriver from the floor. Stevie finds tabs of LSD inside a paperback. 'I want to know where me own stuff is... You took it didn't you? That's how you got the money to pay for the car', Brett says to Glenn. 'You're a dumb prick, aren't you?' Glenn agrees. 'Yeah I am', says Glenn. Stevie and Glenn each take a tab of acid.

The segue from the shaky style of current time to what is now *present time* is seamless—and the image of Brett's face as he looks upon his brothers, perhaps already knowing what is to come, is a mask of normality over unspeakably evil intention.

*

Flash forward: SENTENCING. The three brothers are taken from a prison van into the court house. Police and court officers stand in the darkness of a garage—and the boys appear one at a time...

*

As Sandra tends to Abo's head wounds the boys leave the house. They head out in Stevie's car. Nola—a tiny, forlorn figure seen against the backdrop of a floodlit chemical plant—waits by the side of the road. When the boys arrive at the bottle shop, it is closed. They drive on, listless, their faces white in the green dashboard lights, Stevie and Glenn's eyes wide and black under the influence of the LSD. By chance they pass Nola and Stevie swerves off the road—but when he looks back she has already hitched a lift. Drug-addled, drunk and confused, Stevie's not sure if he'd even seen her. Time seems to be slowing down.

When Stevie lights a cigarette, Brett asks for one. He lights it and inhales heavily. 'Fuck that's good', he says. 'A moment of peace and serenity with me brothers'. Glenn laughs—'It's just been one fucking blue after another'. They all laugh. 'No we're together just the way God planned it', says Brett. 'You

'A moment of peace and serenity with me brothers.'

mean the way you planned it', says Glenn. 'Same thing', says Brett.

A woman walking alone is seen from their moving car.

Stopped in a car park, the lights on Stevie's car go out with a soft clunk. The woman is waiting at a bus stop. There is no-one else around—the streets are deserted. The boys watch her closely. 'That's what we are', says Brett. 'We're all gods. These are the worlds that we've made—Arrakis, Alderaan the Moons of Infinity.' Stevie watches the woman. 'Hey', he says, 'She's looking this way.'

We see the woman standing at a bus stop—alone—vulnerable.

Brett stubs out his cigarette. He thinks for a long moment: 'Let's get her.'

3

YOU ARE HERE

The Boys has recognisably realistic settings of Australian suburban life—the Sprague home, the Fife and Drum bottle shop, the streets and roads around the train station that serve as the setting of the film's disturbing conclusion. Yet the very notion of the visual—and perhaps therefore of *understanding*—are questioned. The film also deploys a number of visual metaphors. The opening titles shift in their focus, suggesting a constricted point of view, a visual metaphor that is repeated throughout the movie—such as when Jackie curls her eye lashes in a mirror as she and Glenn ready themselves to visit the Sprague family home, or as Michelle takes a photo of the family, and most literally and horribly, when Michelle is nearly blinded by Brett during their fight in the laundry.

In keeping with the overall approach of *suggesting* rather than *showing*—and creating considerable tension by doing so—*The Boys* was edited in a highly unconventional style: often the character speaking is not the character seen on screen. As the terrified Nola tries to summon the courage to leave, and tells Sandra and Michelle of her plans, the image stays almost exclusively on Michelle. Nola sits at the kitchen table in profile, presumably watching TV (although we don't know what she's actually looking at, she might just as well be staring blankly into space) and is situated in the middle of the frame, but well back. The bodies of Michelle and Sandra move back and forth across frame as they talk, and we cannot see Nola completely. The camera settles on Michelle as she lights a cigarette. Off screen, Nola says she wants to go, and only then do we see her properly, for the first time in the scene, front on, standing, as she gets up from the table. As Nola relates her poorly thought out plan, we see that Michelle's face is coldly unimpressed, removed from Nola's anguish. When eventually the film cuts back again to Nola, her face is uncertain, weakly smiling but obviously afraid. As the scene progresses and Stevie and Sandra are seen, the cutting for the most part avoids the person speaking to stay on the person listening. It only cuts to the person speaking when a line of dialogue has emotional impact—such as when Stevie violently denies caring about Nola. But most disturbing of all is the moment at the end of the scene when Brett 'comforts' Nola—and her head is cut off by the top of frame. It is a very casual moment in keeping with the rest of the scene but its implications for the narrative make it one of the film's most provocative visual metaphors.

Shots are cluttered with detail, forcing the audience to look around or through things that obscure the action but, more crucially, deprive the audience of a stable point of identification, creating a sense of unease and menace. If it isn't bodies getting in the way, it's parts of the house, doorframes, edges of walls and hallways. In a brief scene where Abo feeds the family dog, we spy him from around the corner of the house, the camera moving around the edge of a wall, the audience forced to feel as though it is we who are moving and looking. This sense of disorientation is reinforced by deep focus combined with sudden camera moves.

When Jackie drives back to the house she parks outside and calls Glenn from her mobile phone. We spy her through the barred windows of the house, in the distance, kept away from the family, physically and emotionally removed. As she finally throws her wedding ring at Glenn and then drives off, the camera spins around to catch Glenn looking at the car before he staggers back into the house. In the scene where Brett and Michelle head to the laundry, they stop first at the corner of the house to kiss and grope one another, the camera flips up and down in slow motion, adding a seasick-like nausea to the moment.

If it were considered only as an audio-visual experience—as an experience separate to its story, performances and narrative—*The Boys* is extraordinary. The production design by Luigi Pittorino keeps the colour range subdued, mute and low key—the colour palate rarely extending into brightness, and when it does—say in the garish orange of a plastic lampshade, the swirls of blue and red on bedroom posters or the blue paint of a door—the cold grain of the image suggests these few bright objects are destined for the side of the road, or a rubbish tip, or to slowly fade and disintegrate. The skin tones of the actors look similarly distressed, white, pallid and too long indoors. The clothes are muted greens, blues and grey. Everything feels drained of life and vitality.

As some critics have noted, *The Boys* is a film with a finely detailed and unified aesthetic designed to keep the audience off balance, disoriented and uncertain.[25] These approaches to the visual schema of the film, from the composition of shots and its editing to its production design and wardrobe, are matched by what is one of the most compelling elements of the film experience—music and sound. The jazz group, The Necks—Chris Abrahams (piano), Tony Buck (drums), and Lloyd Swanton (bass)—composed hours of music that evokes a mood of dread and tension, without clichéd 'dramatic' overstatement.[26] The music is used sparingly, appearing during the titles, segues and the moody *other space* interludes.[27]

The music of the film has been justly celebrated but just as the visual style of the film is the result of a combination of elements, so too is the film's evocative soundtrack. Mixed with the music of The Necks is the composition *Beauty* by 'wire musician' Dr. Alan Lamb, a field recording of the harmonics of the hundreds-of-kilometres-long telephone lines in rural Western Australia. Using contact microphones to record the reverberant low frequency sound, Lamb mixed and composed music from sounds that suggest electronic generation but are instead the eerily beautiful result of interactions of wire with the environment.[28] In the context of *The Boys*, the inclusion of Lamb's work in the mix confuses the identification of *outside* and *inside* sound perspectives, an aural equivalent to the film's visual metaphors. Another fascinating aspect of the film's sound design is the use of altered sound perspectives to heighten otherwise everyday sounds to a disturbing intensity.[29] In the scene where Glenn and Jackie get ready to go the Sprague house, we see Glenn pouring water from a kettle into two cups—the sound perspective of the recording is very close, but Glenn is far from the camera in the kitchen. In another more pointed audio cue, as Brett sits in the back of Stevie's car smoking, deciding on the fate of the innocent woman, the sound of the burning cigarette is delivered with excruciating detail.

These visual and aural metaphors of estrangement match the narrative, where characters continually avoid the problems before them, instead ignoring them or making excuses. When, at the start of the film, Stevie picks up Brett from the prison gates he is carrying a coffee table. It's such a mundane, everyday object yet Stevie asks what it is. When Brett presents the coffee table to his mum, claiming that it's a gift he's made especially for her, Sandra is speechless. These two scenes acknowledge that the characters know that a pretence to normality is just that, a false and doomed attempt.

These efforts are treated with contempt by the other family members, yet each refuses to face their own problems. Nola is living with the family because her own father rejected her when she became pregnant—but Stevie only speaks to her to deny her. Glenn knows he's pushing the limits of his relationship with Jackie when he doesn't go to work nor defends her in front of Brett, yet he does nothing to avoid being sacked or, later, when a choice is demanded between Jackie and his brothers, he cannot act.

Sandra is deeply conflicted. At first loyal to her sons, she says to Michelle that 'there are worse things in the world than my boys' and claims that while at home they will do as she says. Yet when faced with their blatant criminality—when the police arrive at the door, when they are openly derisive of her efforts to maintain a normal family life, or when she displays a breezy dismissal of Brett's time in prison (telling the visiting Nick that Brett has been away on holiday)—Sandra seems unable to act to stop what everyone seems to know is coming—a murderous outburst of inarticulate rage. When Sandra is left alone at the end of the film, with only Abo as a companion, she does the last and only thing she can do—pity her son.

Michelle—despite seeming to be the only character that can stand up to Brett—is compromised by her very involvement with him. The film implies a strength in Michelle's character that seems absent from Nola and Sandra, but as she interacts with Brett—as in the scene where they flirt, or when she tells him he's heading back to prison if he doesn't wise up, or when she tells him he's a loser, Michelle appears to be playing a game. Perhaps she is secretly thrilled by Brett's barely controlled violence, or perhaps she has known him to be different, but at the moment of her final realisation of his true nature—the moment in the laundry when he attacks her—it is also the moment of Brett's impotence. She mocks him, ridicules his masculinity, accusing him of having 'taken it up the arse' in prison. Brett explodes into violence and she is lucky to escape. Later, when Brett is in prison, and he relies on Michelle for an alibi for the murder of the anonymous woman we see at the end of the film, she refuses to see him. Tellingly, Michelle is mute—the last time we see her she is silent, afraid, locked inside the safety of her grandmother's flat.

You're One of Us Now

On that day in 1998 after the preview screening when I called Rowan at home to congratulate him on *The Boys*, there was one thing I knew I wanted to say—namely, how brave I thought it had been to base the story of the film on the murder of Anita Cobby. Rowan was emphatic—the film was *not based* on that famed case.

On 2 February 1986, Anita Cobby, a nurse and former teenage beauty pageant winner, was abducted from a street near Blacktown train station and murdered in a lonely field in Prospect, in Sydney's far western suburbs. Her killers were five men; three brothers—Michael, Gary and Les Murphy—and Michael Murdoch and John Travers. The details of the case, the arrest of the men, and the subsequent trial caused a sensation. The media hysteria was based on the horror provoked by the details of the murder; that she had been chosen at random as the killers had looked for a woman with a handbag they could steal; that her subjection to multiple rapes had escalated into a savage beating and then to her near-decapitation by the leader of the men, John Travers.

What heightened the outrage was an apparent lack of contrition or remorse among the killers. Evidence given during the trial seemed to indicate that these were men with no morals or humanity. Allegations in the tabloid press about Travers piled further horror on to the outrage—a killer of animals, a sodomizer of sheep, a rapist who made no discrimination between men or women, a gang leader who led cowards, a thief, an unemployed monster-at-large, Travers and his co-accused were the worst of the worst.[30] The intensity of the story had morphed into a wider moral panic that touched on many fears and prejudices—the horror of random violence, the hatred of an immoral underclass, and the misogyny of male working-class Australian culture. I think back to that dinner with Catherine in 1986, barely a month after the event, and remember the ferocity of the anger that poured out of people. The murder of Anita Cobby remains an archaeological layer in the public memory of Sydney. You don't have to dig deep to find it.[31]

The screenplay of *The Boys* by Stephen Sewell was based on a play of the same name by Gordon Graham that premiered in Sydney at the Griffin Theatre in 1991. For his part, Graham admits that although the play—and hence the film—was not based directly on the story of Cobby, the event was the 'trigger' for writing it.[32] The film story bears certain undeniable similarities to the case; the three brothers, the images of train stations, Brett burning his clothes (as did Travers), the general working-class milieu of the family. Although these are the primary points of connection between a well-remembered real event and a story that deploys an entirely fictionalised set of circumstances and characters, *The Boys* nonetheless enters into very difficult terrain—the vexed relationship between fiction and reality. Woods' denial of the connection—and subsequent denials by the film's producers, Robert Connolly and John Maynard, as the Australian media began to report this assumption as fact—has been widely disregarded by many who know of the Cobby story. For many, the film *is that story* whether they have seen it or not.

In Sewell's script, the narrative of *The Boys* is a study of the psychotic charm and manipulative power of Brett. Deprived of real power or influence, emasculated not only by women but also by other men, Brett's ambitions have no grounding in real life. Throughout the film, Brett evokes the other worldly powers of space beings—see, for example, the posters in his bedroom of aliens and space craft, his name checks of the planets Arrakis from *Dune* (David Lynch, 1984) and Alderaan from *Star Wars Episode 4: A New Hope* (George Lucas, 1977) and his grandiose view of himself as a God, or a man with the power of a god.[33] For Brett there is *no choice*, a point he makes abundantly clear to his brothers throughout the film. His twisted, self-centred philosophy is contradictory; he is a god, yet he has no choice—and so his ultimate act is to deprive another of her power to live. The violence that ends the film is unseen but powerfully suggested by the detail of the film's narrative. Given everything that has happened in the film, and everything that has been implied about Brett's impotence and frustration, we can assume that the acts against the woman at the bus stop are both sexual—rape and murder. The exact nature of the crimes is left deliberately ambiguous. Since we are left to imagine the worst, it's little wonder then that so many who saw the film in Australia substituted the worst that they could imagine, and her name was Anita Cobby.

The journey of *The Boys* is across a series of internal battlefields; the battle for dominance between Brett, his brothers, Sandra, Michelle and the poor, frightened Nola; the struggle to gain control of what Sewell calls 'Glenn's soul'—the attempts to lay blame for the misery of the characters, either on each other, or on those nebulous others called 'them'—all of this set inside the Sprague home, perhaps substituting, in its particular detail, for the larger Anglo-Irish culture of Australian suburbia.[34] The film's conclusion is bleak; it offers no easy answer, no comforting sense that justice has been done by the arrest and imprisonment of Brett and his brothers. Rather, the unavoidable conclusion is that this sort of violence happens when people lose sight of their morality, when they dispense with all pretence to humanity. The boys end up in jail and the women flee—Jackie from her marriage, Michelle to her grandmother, and Nola to places unknown. Only Sandra is left behind.

4

SWIMMING POOLS

I had driven down to Sydney through bright spring sunshine to see Rowan. Our meeting place was to be the cafe at the Cook & Phillip Swimming Pool, in the centre of Sydney's CBD. He was taking his kids there for a school holiday swimming camp, and so it seemed like a good place to meet. And there was a lot I wanted to ask him. It was almost exactly ten years since *The Boys* had been released.

The film had been a critical success in Australia. 'Stephen Sewell's screenplay... and Woods's (direction) know exactly how much to show—and what not to show—for maximum dramatic effect' wrote film critic David Stratton in *Variety*. He continued:

> Of a flawless cast, I must single out David Wenham, exceptional as the fearful Brett, and Toni Collette giving her best screen performance to date as Michelle. *The Boys* is an almost unbearably tense depiction of the events leading up to a crime.

Stratton is usually a measured and thoughtful critic, so his words were high praise indeed. Other critics weren't so restrained. Online critic Andrew L. Urban stated that the film was '... one of the most powerful, observant and artistically satisfying Australian films ever made', while Craig Matheson said in *Rolling Stone* that the film was 'primal, so severe that your whole body hangs suspended. Few Australian films ever reach these heights'. The film was rewarded with Australian film industry prizes including five Australian Film Institute awards and four Film Critics Circle awards.[35]

The Boys wasn't a financial success. In 1998, the Australian film industry was at the end of a period when movies such as the ballroom-dancing-cross-culture-rom-com *Strictly Ballroom* (Baz Luhrmann, 1992) and the all-ABBA-miming-all-dancing *Muriel's Wedding* (P.J. Hogan, 1994)—not to mention the execrable camp-theatrical-outback-travelogue *The Adventures of Priscilla, Queen of the Desert* (Stephan Elliott, 1994)—had proven to be big hits with Australian audiences.[36] *The Boys* proved too much for mainstream cinema goers and, no doubt put off by the film's dark subject matter, they stayed away. Woods had capitalised on the critical success of the film, not by immediately directing another feature film, but by returning to directing television, notably a dozen or so episodes of the cult science fiction series, *Farscape* (2002–05).

On the cafe table Rowan had copies of the day's newspapers spread out, a coffee and a mobile phone that seemed to be ringing every other moment—new projects were in the works, deals to be done, public relations problems to be handled.

In the decade since *The Boys* release mainstream cinema had become dominated by genre movies—comic book adaptations, TV spin offs, horror movie remakes, animated family movies and just about all the big budget 'high concept' films ready-marketed to an audience who know the 'franchise' or the 'property' before it hits the local multiplex. Even the supposedly non-generic art-house film is now considered a genre. Where did *The Boys* fit into that whole regime? Rowan's view was that the film was a mix of genres that was partly 'social realist'—films typified by British 'kitchen sink' cinema of the '60s such as Karel Reisz's *Saturday Night and Sunday Morning* (1960) or Ken Loach's *Poor Cow* (1968), and later films with a debt to the tradition, movies such as Mike Leigh's savage indictment of contemporary British society in *Naked* (1993) and, especially relevant to *The Boys*, the confronting portrait of English working-class violence, drug addiction and crime in Gary Oldman's *Nil By Mouth* (1997). This was a tradition that *The Boys* seemed to naturally follow—a film that draws its drama not from the sweep of 'action' but from the interplay between its characters. And like these films, *The Boys* did not attempt to answer its own difficult questions; rather it simply depicted them, and offered a portrait of the time.

The other genre Rowan cited was a bit more puzzling—horror. His view was that *The Boys*, in its menace, in its withholding of narrative detail, while creating dread in its suggestion of events to come—not to mention its moody soundtrack and low rumbling audio effects—was explicitly connected to the horror movie tradition. And in a way it is. But something doesn't quite add up. Stephen Sewell claimed that Brett's aspirations to greatness, his yearning for god-like status, were something that lifted the story to a 'metaphysical' level. And indeed *The Boys* is a classical tragedy, albeit one with a contemporary anti-hero at its centre. This tradition follows a fatally flawed character yearning for self realisation through some doomed quest and, in the process, defies the gods while aspiring to their power. Like Hamlet, Brett is without a father, but instead of a throne to reclaim, his sociopathic violence leads him to victimise his family, and the woman he murders. His flaw is the inability to see that he is the author of his own downfall. The foretelling of Brett's ultimate doom is created by the flash forwards, a framing device that Sewell and Woods adapted from Graham's play. We know that Brett and his brothers are doomed, and that they will destroy the family in the process. Sewell referred to Brett's quest as an attempt to reclaim 'his kingdom'. Instead of victory, he is metaphorically dead—in denial, rejected by the world and estranged from it.

The Boys is a remarkable film, not just for what it achieved, but in what it set out do—namely, it wanted to say something. As Sewell put it, behind *The Boys* was 'a massive determination to say something important about Australia, how Australia was, and how Australian men were'.[37] In this regard, *The Boys* stands virtually alone in contemporary Australian cinema. Earlier films of the Australian New Wave as varied as Beresford's social comedy *Don's Party* (1976) or Weir's sci-fi-horror-grotesque-smash-em-up *The Cars That Ate Paris* (1974)—and indeed Kotcheff's groundbreaking *Wake in Fright* (1971)—took the state of Australia and its culture as their bigger themes. Since *The Boys*, few films have attempted anything like its bold combination of classical tragedy, social realism and artfully constructed filmmaking techniques. Even fewer have succeeded.

Many films have attempted to describe the same sort of working-class milieu and have tried to mix similar elements of crime film plotting with social realism. Daniel Krige's *West* (2007), for example, features a desperate cast of characters in the outer reaches of Sydney's suburbia lost under an eerie orange night time sky, evoking *The Boys* eerie *other space* sequences. *West*'s characters sell drugs, plot and double cross each other, all of it seemingly without much purpose or a moral point to make, and the film ends with an absurd and melodramatic conclusion.

More successful by far was Khoa Do's *The Finished People* (2003), an ultra-low-budget, shot-on-video story of young people living on and around the streets of Cabramatta, a suburb of Sydney with a sometimes uneasy and volatile mix of Vietnamese and Anglo-Australian cultures. Feeling at times more like a documentary with its low res images of hoodie-wearing Anglo boys and wan Vietnamese girls trudging the streets, *The Finished People* features interview-style voiceovers from characters explaining their predicaments and elements of crime movie plotting appear as one street kid is tempted by a professional crime gang.[38]

Suburban Mayhem (Paul Goldman, 2006) is the polar opposite of *West* and *The Finished People*, mixing crime with comedy, fantasy and murder in a colour-saturated screen version of otherwise dreary suburban Newcastle. From a script by Alice Bell and featuring an extraordinary performance by Emily Barclay as Katrina Skinner, *Suburban Mayhem* is like the anti-*Boys*—a sociopathic female lead character who twists and messes with male egos for her own ultimate advantage, and at a similar cost to her family. Despite their good intentions and moments of worthy value, these films are not comparable to *The Boys*, either in their delivery or ambition.

The film that bears the closest (if superficial) resemblance to *The Boys* is a film that was released the year before. Steven Vidler's *Blackrock* (1997) was adapted from a stageplay by Nick Enright, who also wrote the screenplay. Although both films use the murder of a young woman as the core event that drives their plots, the two films couldn't be more different in tone and outlook.[39] Set in the beachside surfing culture of Newcastle, *Blackrock* centres on the moral fulminations and inaction of Jared (Laurence Breuls) who is faced with the choice between dobbing in his mate Ricko

(Simon Lyndon) to the police—for rape and murder—or simply doing nothing. *Blackrock*'s pounding rock music soundtrack and bland, unimaginative television-style cinematography give the audience little room to consider its portentous moral questions. Jared does nothing for most of the film and when he finally acts it seems utterly futile. A comparison with *The Boys* is harsh on *Blackrock*. Clearly its makers wanted to say something meaningful but when one thinks of films that take on the bleakest aspects of contemporary suburban life—films such as Tim Hunter's *River's Edge* (1986), Harmony Korine's *Gummo* (1997), or Gus Van Sant's *Elephant* (2003)—it is clear that confronting the violence and distrust at the heart of suburbia can make powerful drama. It seems, however, that most Australian filmmakers are either not brave or talented enough to try—or are pandering to the tastes of the audience in search of a 'hit'.[40]

*

Our conversation drifted from the specifics of *The Boys* and his subsequent movies to other things—the global financial crisis, the film industry, great movies and the stinkers we'd seen, old mutual friends, dream projects—the sort of thing we discussed back in the Super '80s. As we sat in the cafe next to a glass wall, children started walking in from the swimming pool to an outside patio, picking up fruit and juice boxes. 'Those are my two sons', Rowan said, pointing through the glass, 'and that's my daughter'. I could see Rowan's daughter sitting on a concrete step. She had the same red hair and fair skin of her father, but she was sitting in the sun, seemingly unconcerned, an apple in one hand, juice in the other. I talked of my own daughter, Lily, and the distance we'd come.

And then I had a thought—something that was perhaps obvious and had escaped me—but the realisation had the odd clarity of something true.

It isn't about the boys. It is about the girls.

The Beach

I live on a street lined with empty houses. The people who live here are elderly retiree couples, usually seen walking their dogs, ambling down to the local shop for skim milk. The streets are quiet. At night odd house lights can be glimpsed among the trees, blue reflections of televisions in picture windows, no sounds save for the calls of night birds and distant surf.

Then, for twelve weeks a year—those weeks spread out by the seasons of school holidays, long weekends, Christmas and New Year—everything changes and the place is full of people. The normally vacant beach houses are bursting with partying teenagers and young families enjoying the pleasures of the beach. Roadsides are crowded with parked four wheel drives, luxury sedans and monster pleasure boats on trailers. The quiet is split by the sounds of music, fast cars screaming along slow streets, the beat of chart music.

The beach is an anomaly on this part of the New South Wales coast just 110 kilometres north of Sydney. There are examples of conspicuous wealth in other residential zones, in retirement cloisters such as Hardy's Bay and Copacabana, but here it's different, physically separated from the rest of the Central Coast by a mountain, a headland and the dense forest of a National Park. And there's the ocean. When you arrive, it feels as though there is no reason to leave. That is until you run out of food, or want to go to the movies, or post a letter or do something that requires contact with the world. And that takes you into direct contact with the working-class suburbs of nearby Woy Woy, Umina and Ettalong.

I've been on the Coast for six years now. I'd lived in various suburbs around inner-city Sydney for close to a quarter of a century and the idea of moving out of the city was a strange notion. I'd holidayed in Pearl Beach since I was a kid, but to live here, full time, all year round?

In 1982 I had fled the suburbs of north-western Sydney for the arty bohemia of the inner city. I liked the idea of having 'culture' just down the street from my house—cinemas, art galleries, bars, bookshops and cafes—and it was a lifestyle I hung on to for decades. Rachel and I were married in 1994 and we rented an apartment in Woolloomooloo. Then we moved up the hill to Darlinghurst. We were inner-city people. Or so I thought. I had become exhausted by Sydney and hadn't even known it. A move to a beach side suburb, a sort of modest 'sea change', felt like an option worth exploring. The idea was that we'd be out of Sydney for six months, to see how it went, and then go back. But we stayed.

One day, while I was smoking a cigarette, drinking a coffee and enjoying the morning sunshine on my balcony, I realised something had changed. It was no longer a choice. I simply couldn't go back. I had fled the burbs, but now I was back, albeit in the regional ambience of a fringe community on the edge of what is euphemistically called 'Greater Sydney'.

Living on the Coast provided me with a rich and exotic insight into an Australia that I had forgotten. I became an avid reader of the local newspaper and clipped stories. There was a classic tale in the *Peninsula News* of a haunted picnic table in a local beer garden that had inexplicably bucked into the air at the mention of deceased drinker during a long drinking session. It turned out that the late gentleman had built the very wooden table at which the party was seated: a sign from beyond the grave was the only logical explanation. There was the story of the lower half of a set of dentures that had washed up on Ocean Beach in Umina. Accompanying a photo of the beach at sunset, the caption advised possible owners of the dentures to contact the editor. And there was the front page story of the British High Consul's visit to a pie factory in Gosford. A large photo showed the Consul tucking into a pie in front of a pie-vending machine with two buttons—one for PIE, the other for PIE WITH SAUCE.

And then there were the other stories. One was about a girl who'd got off her regular school bus on the way home. A boy came up to her, spoke to her for a second… and then stabbed her repeatedly. As she lay dying by the side of the road she told the police the identity of her killer—a boy who lived down the road from her house. Another was about a guy who had served with the Australian army in East Timor. He walked into the Woy Woy Bowling Club, said his backpack was filled with explosives and then went outside to wait for the police to arrive. It turned out he thought he'd lost all his money and, although he didn't have any explosives in his backpack, or had even lost the money, he was trying to provoke a situation where the cops would shoot him. 'Death by cop', they call it. And there was an incident late one night when a man walking to the train station in Ourimbah asked two boys what they were doing out on the street at nearly midnight. He had his head staved in by a letter box wielded by one of the kids.

Sometimes the stories are closer to home. Two teenagers rode their push bikes around the cliff path from the caravan park in Umina into Pearl Beach. They stopped at the shop where the owner's elderly, dotty mother was in charge that day. The teenagers saw their chance when the old woman stood for a long, lingering moment, lost in thought as she counted change over an open register drawer. They grabbed the cash and made off on their bikes. The shop owner chased after them in the shop's truck, cornering them near the Umina caravan park. The two kids, trapped, turned and bashed the owner into unconsciousness, splitting his skull, fracturing bones and nearly killing him.

These incidents of violence aren't common on the Coast. They make the local news because they are unusual. Moments of exception. The violence appears lurid, grotesquely outlined by the seeming normality of their context. Reading the stories, knowing the places where they had taken place, is like a flash gun popping in your eyes on a bright sunny day. All this happens *here*. It wasn't as though I hadn't witnessed violence where I'd lived in Sydney. I'd seen people bashed by bouncers outside clubs and knife fights on Bondi Beach. My friends had stepped over the inert corpses of junkies lying in their doorways. And one day my partner, Rachel, and I had seen the body of Czech backpacker in Kings Cross who'd been killed by an axe blow to the face. But that was the city, and somehow I had accepted it.

The retreat to the Coast was supposed to be an escape from all that. But it turns out that life and death are everywhere.

NOTES

1   John Lindsay was an actor in various Super 8 movies during the mid '80s. He was later the co-host of SBS's one-off 1999 TV show *Cooking with Frank*, directed by Catherine Lowing.

2   And I can still quote you large chunks of dialogue with a few drinks under the belt.

3   The Institute is now known as the UNSW College of Fine Arts.

4   Nick, Sean and I met at a young filmmakers workshop held at the Sydney Filmmakers' Cooperative around 1979. We were like-minded teenagers with a love of surreal and absurd comedy, cult and classic films. We collaborated on various creative projects including films, music and radio shows for more than a decade. Sean made numerous short films and documentaries, and founded *The Tender Trap*—a club at the forefront of the early '90s Easy Listening revival—and is now a maker of experimental radio and video art installations. He served as a music consultant on *The Boys*. Nick is a respected film editor and creative consultant on numerous features and short films.

5   *Wake In Fright* was remastered and re-released in late 2009. Tina Kaufman has written a monograph on the film in this Series to be published in winter, 2010.

6   *Wake in Fright* was shot in Broken Hill, another dusty township in regional New South Wales.

7   For more on some of these films please see *Alvin Purple* by Catharine Lumby, *The Adventures of Barry McKenzie* by Tony Moore, and *The Devil's Playground* by Christos Tsiolkas—all in the Australian Screen Classics series, co-published by Currency Press and the National Film & Sound Archive.

8   The late '70s were the golden years of art-house cinema with numerous well-attended venues around Sydney. Their distribution role is now largely taken up by specialist DVD labels and the chance to see these kinds of films in a cinema is now restricted to cinematheques in Brisbane and Melbourne.

9   This punning term was coined by Super 8 filmmaker and writer/journalist Michael Hutak, to ironically comment on the relentlessly optimistic boosterism of Sydney's underground film scene in the 1980s. A retrospective of '80s Super 8 film culture at the Museum of Contemporary Art in 1999, curated by Sean O'Brien, took it as the exhibition's title.

10 In fact, its limitations were theorised into something called 'the Super 8 effect'. The emergent Super 8 film culture of the early to mid '80s was adopted by film critics and art theorists such as Edward Colless, Rex Butler and Adrian Martin who, among others, helped create a sense of a genuine cultural movement.

11 The SS8FG still exists—sort of... In the late '80s the group became the Sydney Intermedia Network after an amalgamation with the Sydney Video Festival. In the '90s, again under new management, the group morphed into d/Lux/MediaArts. See: http://www.dlux.org.au/cms/index.php?/d/Archive.html

12 There was of course the Sydney Film Festival, and the Dendy Awards, with its highly contested categories for short and 'long short' narrative, animated and experimental films. In the period from the late '70s until the early '90s, the Dendy was dominated by student films from the Australian Film & TV School, creating the feeling that only certain kinds of films would be screened.

13 Our films were produced under the collective name 'The Marine Biologists'.

14 *The Big Lunch* screened as part of the SFF in 1988.

15 A few uncredited grabs from *It's All True* can be glimpsed in the making-of documentary on *The Boys* DVD (Madman, 2004).

16 *Summer in the City* (1970) and *Alice in the Cities* (1974) had already confirmed Wenders' international star status but his relationship with Sydney in the 1980s made him a cult figure. After a visit to the SFF with *Paris, Texas* in 1984 Wenders later secured co-funding for *Until the End of the World* (1991) from the Australian Film Commission. He was spotted in and around Sydney for many years, once memorably with his then-girlfriend, the actress Solveig Dommartin, wandering lost in a city shopping arcade. Aside from Woods's Wenders-parodying *Suspect Filmmaker*, Sean O'Brien and Catherine Lowing would later make *Brutini* (1990), a short film featuring a German-accented character named Solveig, a tribute to the hold that Wenders had over our imaginations.

17 Super 8 Film Festivals from 1983 until 1987 were staged over several nights and days at the Chauvel Cinema in Paddington, Sydney, and would often feature as many as 20+ films per session, with sell-out crowds coming to see their friend's films, to cheer and laugh—or loudly ridicule

the efforts of unknowns. The intensity of these screenings prompted Ted Colless to describe the sessions as a 'theatre of cruelty'.

18 A location that would be revisited in his second feature film *Little Fish* (2005).

19 Simon von Wolkenstein, a designer and friend also first met at the Sydney Filmmakers' Cooperative, shot most of our collaborative movies including *The Big Lunch* (1988). Working as a designer, filmmaker and director, Simon also directed the TV special *The Art Life at the Biennale of Sydney* (ABC, 2008) and the second series of *The Art Life* (ABC, 2009).

20 *Tran The Man* is included as a bonus feature on the Madman DVD of *The Boys*.

21 *Tran The Man* is a fascinating companion piece to *The Boys*—many its key crew worked on the later feature including Nick Meyers (editor), Sam Petty (sound design), Tristan Milani (camera operator) and Janet Merewether (title design)—and uses some of the techniques that would be explored in *The Boys*, such as sequences shot on video and then refilmed, crowded frame composition and an experimental sound design and music mix.

22 The *flash forward* is a rarely used film narrative technique that shows events that will happen in the future. In *The Boys* these flash forwards are indicated by a noticeably different visual style, and each sequence is titled with a time frame, such as EIGHTEEN HOURS LATER. This approach, although initially confusing, becomes more explicable as the film progresses. At the time of its release *The Boys* was notable for its approach to constructing multiple time frames in the overall narrative and remains one of the few films to use the flash forward device. However, since its release, a number of films have attempted non-linear structures for their films, offering complex multiple narrative time frames, such as Alejandro González Iñárritu's *21 Grams* (2003), or radically altered time flows, such as Christopher Nolan's story-told-in-reverse *Memento* (2000).

23 These and other insert sequences in the film were shot on Hi 8, a low grade '80s-era home video format.

24 The film's title sequence was designed by filmmaker, art director and production designer Janet Merewether. After shooting hours of footage on videotape on the empty sets, a video storyboard was compiled for the sequence, later re-shot on film by Woods and crew. The conceptual

framework for the sequence was to represent in abstract visuals the point of view of the film's main character, Brett Sprague (David Wenham). See Andrew Frost, *Name Behind The Title*, Monument 30, June/July, 1999.

25 See for example Fiona A. Villella, 'The Boys', in *Senses of Cinema*, http://archive.sensesofcinema.com/contents/00/9/symposium.html#4

26 The band visited the set of the film during production and after extensive discussions with Woods recorded music without reference to any visuals. See *The Boys* DVD (Madman, 2004). Nominated Best Soundtrack Album, ARIA Awards and Australian Guild of Screen Composers Award, the music is available on CD as *Music For The Feature Film 'The Boys'*, Wild Sound/MDS 1998, Reissued 2004 Fish of Milk. http://www.thenecks.com/pages/cds.html

27 The band's *Black* CD was played on set during the film's extensive rehearsal period to evoke mood and tone.

28 For more on Lamb and his work, see for example Cabinet Magazine #3 http://www.cabinetmagazine.org/art/cds/squall.php and Andrew McLennan, *A Brief Topology of Australian Sound Art & Experimental Broadcasting*, http://www.kunstradio.at/

AUSTRALIA/lennon_topology.htm

29 Mixed by veteran sound engineer Phil Judd, *The Boys* also featured the effects editing of Sam Petty, who would take the role of sound designer on films with exquisitely detailed soundscapes, including Woods's *Little Fish* (2005), *The Bank* (Robert Connolly, 2001), *Romulus, My Father* (Richard Roxburgh, 2007) and many others.

30 For a sample of the kind of reporting that has been prompted by the case, see *The Murder of Anita Cobby: Australia's Worst Crime*, http://www.trutv.com/library/crime/notorious_murders/young/cobby/1.html

31 An interesting side story to *The Boys* is the work of artist Adam Cullen. In 2000 Cullen won the Archibald Prize for Portraiture with a rendering of David Wenham. Although nominally a portrait of an actor, Cullen has had a long fascination with crime and criminality, and stated to this author that in his mind at least, the portrait was of Brett Sprague, not the actor. Later, Cullen took part in a group show *Anita and Beyond* in 2003 staged at Penrith Regional Gallery, a show organised to commemorate the Cobby story. Cullen contributed five individual portraits of the killers.

32 See *The Boys* DVD (Madman, 2004). Like *The Boys* as a film, the play was dogged by controversy, from an initial reading at a playwright's conference to its first staging.

33 Not coincidentally perhaps, both *Dune* and *Star Wars* are stories of messianic figures who rise up against oppression, destroy corrupt authority figures, avenge the deaths of their fathers and achieve their destiny through violent, decisive action.

34 Hear Sewell's comments on the film's thematic concerns in the making-of documentary on *The Boys* DVD (Madman, 2004).

35 Australian Film Institute Awards: Rowan Woods (Best Achievement in Direction), Toni Collette (Best Supporting Actress), John Polson (Best Supporting Actor), and Stephen Sewell (Best Adapted Screenplay), an Australian Screen Sound Guild Award for Best Achievement in Location Recording for a Feature Film, Film Critics Circle of Australia Awards for Rowan Woods (Best Director), Lynette Curran (Best Supporting Actress), and Stephen Sewell (Best Adapted Screenplay).

36 For a hilariously funny and scathing critique of *Priscilla, Queen of the Desert*, see Philip Brophy's Australian Screen Classics edition on this film.

37 Stephen Sewell on *The Boys* DVD (Madman, 2004).

38 The similarities of *The Finished People*'s suburban setting and thematic approaches to *The Boys* may have been a conscious one as Woods subsequently appeared in the role of 'Snake Pit Leader' in Do's later football-fans-gone-wrong feature *Footy Legends* (2006).

39 Enright's play and subsequent film script was based in part on the rape and murder of a teenager named Leigh Leigh in Stockton, near Newcastle, in November 1989.

40 This is not to say that in the last decade there haven't been any decent Australian films. *Noise* (Matthew Saville, 2007) is a notable film in the crime genre, and there have been the occasional non-genre films such as Cate Shortland's beautiful coming-of-age film *Somersault* (2004) and Ana Kokkinos's harrowingly brilliant *Head On* (1998), but for the most part the film industry has produced competently-made if uninspiring crime dramas such as *The Square* (Nash Edgerton, 2008), yet more Aussie comedies like *Kenny* (Clayton Jacobson, 2006) and even the occasional blockbuster-crime-against-culture-catastrophe that was *Australia* (Baz Luhrmann, 2008).

BIBLIOGRAPHY

Butterss, Philip. 'When being a man is all you've got: Masculinity in Romper Stomper, Blackrock, Idiot Box and The Boys' Metro Magazine #117, 1998. pp 40-46.

Carroll, David. 'The Boys (Review 2001)'. *Tabula Rasa*. Accessed Sept. 28, 2009. http://www.tabula-rasa.info/AusHorror/Boys.html

Craven, Ian. *Australian Cinema in the 1990s*. London: F. Cass. 2001.

Elder, Catriona. *Being Australian: Narratives of National Identity*. Sydney: Allen & Unwin. 2007.

Falcon, Richard. 'The Boys.' *Sight and Sound*, Nov. 1998. pp 43.

Jorgensen, Darren. 'The New Australian Realism.' *Metro Magazine #146/147*. pp 146

Stephens, Tony. 'Minimalist Menace: The Necks Score *The Boys'*. La Trobe University, *Screening The Past*. Accessed Sept. 28, 2009. http://www.latrobe.edu.au/screeningthepast/firstrelease/fr_18/TMfr18a.html

Stratton, David. 'The Boys'. Variety, Feb 23, 1998. pp78.

Sewell, Stephen. *The Boys: Original screenplay based on the original play by Gordon Graham*. Sydney: Currency Press. 1998.

Thomas, David. 'Extraordinary Undercurrents: Australian Cinema, Genre and the Everyday'. PhD Dissertation. Murdoch University, 2006.

Urban, Andrew L. 'Rowan Woods: The Boys DVD'. *Urban Cine File*, November 6, 2003. Accessed Sept, 28, 2009. http://www.urbancinefile.com.au/home/view.asp?a=8111&s=interviews

(Uncredited author). 'Darkness of The Soul'. Time International, May 11, 1998, pp 64.

Villella, Fiona A. 'The Boys'. Senses of Cinema: Contemporary Australian Cinema, A Symposium. Accessed Sept. 28, 2009. http://archive.senseofcinema.com/contents/00/9/symposium.html#4

FILMOGRAPHY

The Adventures of Barry McKenzie, Bruce Beresford, 1972

The Adventures of Priscilla, Queen of the Desert, Stephan Elliott, 1994

Alice in the Cities, Wim Wenders, 1974

Alvin Purple, Tim Burstall, 1973

Alvin Rides Again, David Bilcock & Robin Copping, 1974

Amores Perros, Alejandro González Iñárritu, 2000

Apocalypse Now, Francis Ford Coppola, 1979

The Art Life 2 (TV), Simon von Wolkenstein, 2009

The Art Life at the Biennale of Sydney (TV), Simon von Wolkenstein, 2008

Australia, Baz Luhrmann, 2008

The Bank, Robert Connolly, 2001

Barry McKenzie Holds His Own, Bruce Beresford, 1974

The Big Lunch (Super 8), The Marine Biologists, 1988

Blackrock, Steven Vidler, 1997

Brutini, Catherine Lowing and Sean O'Brien, 1990

The Cars That Ate Paris, Peter Weir, 1974

Cooking With Frank (TV), Catherine Lowing, 1999

Crocodile Dundee, Peter Faiman, 1986

The Devil's Playground, Fred Schepisi, 1976

Dirty Harry, Don Siegel, 1971

Don's Party, Bruce Beresford, 1976

Dune, David Lynch, 1984

Edge of Nowhere (Super 8), The Marine Biologists, 1985

Elephant, Gus Van Sant, 2003

Empire, Andy Warhol, 1964

Eraserhead, David Lynch, 1977

Farscape (TV), 1999–2003

The Finished People, Khoa Do, 2003

40,000 Horsemen, Charles Chauvel, 1940

The F.J. Holden, Mike Thornhill, 1977

Footy Legends, Khoa Do, 2006

Freaks, Tod Browning, 1932

Goodfellas, Martin Scorsese, 1990

Gummo, Harmony Korine, 1997

Head On, Ana Kokkinos, 1998

Heartbreak High (TV), 1994-99

It's All True (Super 8), The Marine Biologists, 1988

Johnny Guitar, Nicholas Ray, 1954

Kenny, Clayton Jacobson, 2006

Kenny's Love (Super 8), Rowan Woods, 1984 1987

La planète sauvage (Fantastic Planet), René Laloux, 1973

Little Fish, Rowan Woods, 2005

Long Weekend, Colin Eggleston, 1978

Love My Way (TV), 2004–07

Mad Max 2, George Miller, 1981

The Man Who Fell to Earth, Nicolas Roeg, 1976

Mean Streets, Martin Scorsese, 1973

Memento, Christopher Nolan, 2000

Meshes of the Afternoon, Maya Deren and Alexander Hammid, 1943

Mickey One, Arthur Penn, 1965

Monkey Grip, Ken Cameron, 1982

Muriel's Wedding, P.J. Hogan, 1994

My Brilliant Career, Gillian Armstrong, 1979

Nashville, Robert Altman, 1975

Naked, Mike Leigh, 1993

Nil By Mouth, Gary Oldman, 1997

Noise, Matthew Saville, 2007

One Plus One, Jean-Luc Godard, 1968

Paris, Texas, Wim Wenders, 1984

Performance, Donald Cammell, 1970

Picnic at Hanging Rock, Peter Weir, 1975

Police Rescue (TV), 1991-1996

Poor Cow, Ken Loach, 1968

Reaction Football (Super 8), Rowan Woods, 1982

River's Edge, Tim Hunter, 1986

Ropo's Movie Nite (Super 8), The Marine Biologists, 1986

Romulus, My Father, Richard Roxburgh, 2007

Saturday Night and Sunday Morning, Karel Reisz, 1960

Scarface, Brian De Palma, 1983

The Secret Life of Us (TV), 2001-06

Sleep, Andy Warhol, 1963

Smiley Gets A Gun, Anthony Kimmins, 1958

Somersault, Cate Shortland, 2004

The Square, Nash Edgerton, 2008

Star Wars Episode 4: A New Hope, George Lucas, 1977

The State of Things, Wim Wenders, 1982

Strictly Ballroom, Baz Luhrmann, 1992

Suburban Mayhem, Paul Goldman, 2006

Summer in the City, Wim Wenders, 1970

Summerfield, Ken Hannam, 1977

Sunday Too Far Away, Ken Hannam, 1975

Suspect Filmmaker, Rowan Woods, 1984

The State of Things, Wim Wenders, 1982

Taxi Driver, Martin Scorsese, 1976

There Will Be Blood, Paul Thomas Anderson, 2007

Three Days of the Condor, Sydney Pollack, 1975

THX 1138, George Lucas, 1971

Tokyo-Ga, Wim Wenders, 1985

Tran the Man, Rowan Woods, 1994

21 Grams, Alejandro González Iñárritu, 2003

Until the End of the World, Wim Wenders, 1991

Wake In Fright, Ted Kotcheff, 1971

West, Daniel Krige, 2007

Winged Creatures, Rowan Woods, 2008

CREDITS

Key Cast

Brett
David Wenham

Stevie
Anthony Hayes

Glenn
John Polson

Jackie
Jeanette Cronin

Nola
Anna Lise

Sandra
Lynette Curran

Abo
Pete Smith

Michelle
Toni Collette

Graham Newman
Peter Hehir

Nick
Sal Sharah

Sparrow
Andrew Heys

Key Crew

Director
Rowan Woods

Producers
Robert Connolly &
John Maynard

Associate Producers
David Wenham,
Douglas Cummins

Script
Stephen Sewell, based
upon the play by
Gordon Graham

**Director of
Photography**
Tristan Milani

Editor
Nick Meyers

Music
The Necks

Titles Design
Janet Merewether

Production Design
Luigi Pittorino